Voices from Shanghai

Voices from Shanghai

JEWISH EXILES IN WARTIME CHINA

Edited, Translated, & with an Introduction by Irene Eber

The University of Chicago Press   Chicago & London

IRENE EBER is the Louis Frieberg Professor of East Asian Studies Emeritus at Hebrew University of Jerusalem. She is the author of many books, including *The Choice: Poland, 1939–1945.*

The University of Chicago Press, Chicago 60637
The University of Chicago Press, Ltd., London
© 2008 by The University of Chicago
All rights reserved. Published 2008
Printed in the United States of America

17 16 15 14 13 12 11 10 09 08   1 2 3 4 5

ISBN-13: 978-0-226-18166-0 (cloth)
ISBN-10: 0-226-18166-9 (cloth)

Frontispiece: "Lane in Hongkou, ca. 1944" (4648/39). Courtesy H. P. Eisfelder Photography Collection (now housed at Yad Vashem Archives, Jerusalem).

Library of Congress Cataloging-in-Publication Data

Voices from Shanghai : Jewish exiles in wartime China / edited, translated, and with an introduction by Irene Eber.
       p.   cm.
    Includes bibliographical references and index.
    ISBN-13: 978-0-226-18166-0 (cloth : alk. paper)
    ISBN-10: 0-226-18166-9 (cloth : alk. paper)
    1. Jews—China—Shanghai—History—Sources. 2. Refugees, Jewish—China—Shanghai—History—Sources. 3. Shanghai (China)—Ethnic relations—Sources. I. Eber, Irene, 1929–
    DS135.C5V65 2008
    940.53′181420951132—dc22

                                                                      2008009646

Maps by Dick Gilbreath and Eric Truesdell at the University of Kentucky Cartography Lab.

FOR MY COLLEAGUES & FRIENDS

Harold Z. Schiffrin, Elli Joffe, and Avraham Altman

Contents

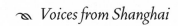 *Voices from Shanghai*

1. Shanghai row houses (aerial view). From
Tess Johnston and Deke Erh, *A Last Look:
Western Architecture in Old Shanghai* (Hong
Kong: Old China Hand Press, 1993), p. 12.
By permission of Deke Erh.

2. Shanghai row house (front). From Tess
Johnston and Deke Erh, *A Last Look: Western
Architecture in Old Shanghai* (Hong Kong: Old
China Hand Press, 1993), p. 12. By permis-
sion of Deke Erh.

Introduction

Shoshana Kahan hated Shanghai from the moment she set foot in it. After only three days in the city, in October 1941, she wrote in her diary, "What a disgusting city Shanghai is . . . now I understand why everyone fought with all their might to remain in Japan. . . . Now I understand the terrible letters we received from those who had the misfortune to be sent here. A dirty disgusting city. . . . "[1]

Annemarie Pordes, on the other hand, immediately fell in love with Shanghai: "It was impossible not to love it at first sight. . . . There was the main road with houses built in Western style and right behind it were small Chinese huts, built . . . of rough stone, clay, or just bamboo. . . . They provided living quarters for human beings, their pigs and chickens, all under one roof. What struck me most was the variety of vehicles: trams, buses, cars, carts drawn by water buffalo, bicycles, and in between, weaving in and out, a large number of rickshaws."[2]

To better understand these two reactions and the fact that European exiles, expatriates, refugees—whatever we want to call them—could not remain indifferent to the metropolis, let me briefly recapitulate some earlier events and explain how large numbers of Jews came to be in Shanghai between 1939 and 1941.

Hitler assumed power in January 1933. Only four months later began the persecution of Jewish professionals. It was, no doubt, the loss of position and income that caused a number of physicians, surgeons, dentists, and pharmacists to decide to go to Shanghai; by December 1933 thirty Jewish families had already presumably arrived.[3] Not all remained in Shanghai, however, and some settled in Guangzhou (Canton), Tianjin, and Qingdao. Still others, like Leo Karfunkel, a dentist, was granted Chinese citizenship some years later and settled in Nanjing.[4]

These professionals had become relatively well established by the time

3. "Car with one horse power, 1942" (4648/8). Courtesy H. P. Eisfelder Photography Collection (now housed at Yad Vashem Archives, Jerusalem).

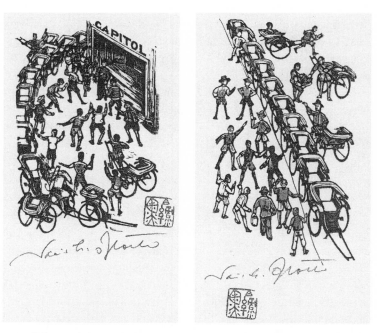

4. "Rickshaw, rickshaw, rickshaw. . . . " From Barbara Hoster et al., eds., *David Ludwig Bloch, Holzschnitte, Woodcuts, Shanghai, 1940–1949* (Sankt Augustin: Monumenta Serica Institute, 1997), pp. 112 and 113. Used by special permission of David Ludwig Bloch / Lydia Abel; all rights reserved.

of the Austrian annexation (Anschluss) in March 1938, and the "night of shattered glass" (Kristallnacht) in November 1938, events that led to a hurried exodus from Central Europe of thousands of people to other parts of the world, including Shanghai. Now not only professionals like doctors and dentists sought to escape as a result of Germany's policy of forced emigration. Shopkeepers, clerks, salesmen of various kinds, actors, journalists, and writers—everyone who had the price of a train or steamship ticket and who could procure a visa—left. Among the throng were also non-Jews, communists, and especially men who had been incarcerated in concentration camps. Evidence of a ticket or visa to another country obtained their release in accordance with a directive by Reinhard Heydrich (1904–1942), which stipulated that a detainee had to be in possession of emigration papers in order to be released.[5] But they had to leave the country within a few days; sometimes within hours.

Whereas the majority of the German and Austrian refugees arrived in Shanghai by sea (mostly from Italian ports until 1940, when Italy joined the war), the Polish refugees came via an overland route. By summer 1941, when the Germans invaded Soviet Russia, this route, too, was no longer accessible, so that emigration to China both by sea and by land was effectively cut off.

Let us now take a closer look at both Shanghai and the Jewish refugees in order to better understand their reaction to the city and its complexities, and their creative responses written in Shanghai about Shanghai translated in these pages. Not only do these poems, letters, prose pieces, and diary entries form an important chapter in exile literature generally, they also tell us something about cultural self-perception and perception of the other.

International Shanghai

The Shanghai that the Central Europeans came to between 1938 and 1941 was, in Frederic Wakeman's words, "one of the most intricate and complicated urban societies in the world."[6] It became this way by stages, having developed for centuries as a walled town and a thriving junk port, the meeting point of Chinese traders from various parts of the empire and southeast Asia. This was all changed by the Opium Wars (1839–1842), following which the Western powers created the so-called treaty system by opening major Chinese cities to foreign trade. In the

1. Major cities and ports for Jewish refugees en route to Shanghai via ship or train.

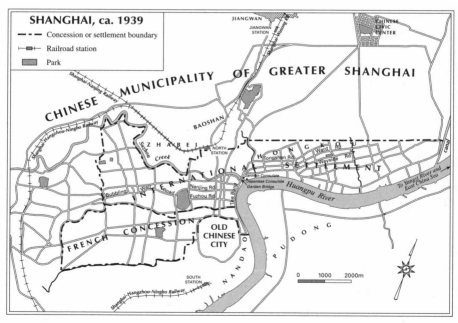

2. Shanghai (ca. 1939).

5. The Gubbay House in the former French Concession, residence of the Sassoon merchant family. From Tess Johnston and Deke Erh, *A Last Look: Western Architecture in Old Shanghai* (Hong Kong: Old China Hand Press, 1993), p. 17. By permission of Deke Erh.

nineteenth and twentieth centuries Shanghai developed rapidly as a major shipping center and a point of vast import and export trade.

Suburbs grew up outside the walled town: the International Settlement and the French Concession (fig. 5), as well as the Chinese areas of Zhabei, Pudong, and Nantao. Not only Westerners flocked to the city in search of new opportunities, but Chinese, too, Ningbo and Zhejiang merchants, and laborers from the coastal provinces. The Taiping rebellion (1850–1864) brought thousands of refugees to Shanghai in search of safety. At the conclusion of the rebellion, more than 110,000 Chinese had moved into the International Settlement and French Concession.[7] In short, Shanghai developed and grew into a modern metropolis as a city of immigrants, both Western and Chinese. Increasingly, as the years wore on, many Europeans no longer considered themselves temporary residents. Shanghai was home, and they planned to remain there.

Yet the city did not develop as a unified urban complex, but was fragmented into several interlocking and interrelated areas with their own administrations. The International Settlement was governed by the Shanghai Municipal Council (SMC), which in time came to be composed of British, American, Chinese, and Japanese officials. It was, however, not a sovereign body; its responsibilities were administrative, and it received its directives from the home governments through their consular bodies. The French Concession was governed by the French Consul General, who derived his authority directly from the French government. After July 1927, the Chinese Nationalist government, with its seat in Nanjing, created the Chinese Municipal Administration responsible for governing the Chinese areas.[8]

By the 1930s, Shanghai's population had grown to more than 3.5 million. Of these, Europeans and Americans formed but a very small percentage, although at its height more than fifty different nationalities were represented in Shanghai's foreign community. By far, the most numerous were the Russian and Japanese communities. White Russian refugees started arriving in Shanghai shortly after the Bolshevik revolution. By 1929, more than 13,000 had come, and this number grew to 25,000 by 1939.[9] In contrast to the Russians, the Japanese were not a refugee community, and in the course of time they came to form the largest foreign community in Shanghai. Despite repatriation in times of conflict and fighting between Japanese and Chinese, the Japanese population soared to 15,551 in 1920 and 54,308 in 1939.[10] Each of these communities lived in distinct areas of the city: the Russians in the French Concession, the British and Americans in the International Settlement, and the Japanese in Hongkou, which was actually an extension of the International Settlement across the Suzhou Creek. The Central European refugees, when they arrived in 1938 and 1939, came to live in Hongkou, often among the Japanese population, because, for the most part, rents were cheaper there than in the International Settlement.

Until the arrival of the Central Europeans, Shanghai's Jewish communities were among the smaller ones in the city. Sephardi (or Baghdadi, as they are also called) Jews arrived on the heels of the British. Not all hailed from Iraq. Most came via Bombay, where they had prosperous business firms, and their aim in Shanghai was to establish branches in the newly opened treaty port. By 1862, a small Jewish community had come into being in which the Sassoon family (see fig. 5, above) began to play a major role.[11] In addition, Silas Aaron Hardoon (1851?–1931), one of Shanghai's most successful landowners, was said to own most of the properties along the famous Nanking Road. According to some accounts, he was the richest foreigner in East Asia at the time of his death.[12] The Baghdadis boasted more wealthy families than any other Jewish community in Shanghai, which was quite out of proportion to their size, for they never seem to have numbered more than approximately 1,000 persons. Upper-class Baghdadis took readily to Western ways, spoke English, and lived in the International Settlement.

The earliest Russian Jewish arrivals probably date from the Russo-Japanese War (1904–1905), after which Jewish conscripts who had been in the Russian army decided to remain in China. But the largest number of Russian Jews, along with some Polish Jews, arrived only after the Russian October Revolution of 1917. By the 1930s, between 6,000 and 7,000 Russian Jews were in Shanghai. Together with the Baghdadis, there were around 8,000 Jews among approximately 50,000 foreigners. Whereas some Baghdadi families were highly affluent, the Russian Jews consisted largely of refugees who were far less wealthy. They had fled from the upheavals of civil war and revolution in Central Asia, and many had drifted south from Harbin in Heilongjiang province. They were, moreover, Russian-speaking Ashkenazi Jews, culturally different from the Sephardis.

The 18,000 to 20,000 German- and Yiddish-speaking refugees, who arrived between 1938 and 1941, were not only destitute in every sense of the word, but were also culturally different from the two established Jewish communities in Shanghai. It may well be that the need to assert their cultural difference (rather than their solidarity) had a role in the cultural activities that will be described further on. Before taking up that topic, however, let me take a brief look at Chinese Shanghai.

Chinese Shanghai

Often referred to as the "Paris of the Orient," Shanghai was primarily a modern manufacturing and business emporium where a new urban class—an intelligentsia, a business and working class—originated.[13] The city was both a capitalist and a cultural center, which had more institutions of higher education than Beijing, and though it was not considered the intellectual center Beijing was, neither was it solely devoted to business and money.

Shanghai had a large publishing industry, both foreign and Chinese, hundreds of printing presses, and a number of Chinese- and English-language dailies. The first modern Chinese newspaper, *Shenbao*, was published in Shanghai from 1872 on. Important modern writers like Mao Dun (Shen Yanping, 1896–1981), Yu Dafu (1896–1945), and Lu Xun (Zhou Shuren, 1891–1936) made Shanghai their home for shorter or longer periods of time, and bookstores along Fuzhou and Henan Roads were a major attraction. A thriving motion picture industry and a large number of movie theaters were another modern novelty of the urban scene. In Shanghai a person could see the latest Hollywood productions as well as films produced in Shanghai studios. The movie house, writes Leo Lee, "created both the material conditions and a cultural climate for movie going as a new habit of urban life."[14]

Although largely unaware of the degree to which Shanghai produced and consumed modern culture, the refugees could not remain unaffected by this unique environment. That they in a short time, too, printed newspapers (fig. 6), produced plays (fig. 7), and created a coffeehouse culture (fig. 8) was, of course, due to the cultural baggage they brought with them. But it was, no doubt, also due to the fact that in Shanghai it was possible to do so.

Shanghai, the Sino-Japanese War, and Its Aftermath

Life was by no means simple and easy, however, and matters grew steadily more complicated as a result of the Sino-Japanese hostilities. Manchuria (Manzhuguo) may have seemed far away when the Japanese attacked and occupied the three northeastern provinces of Liaoning, Jilin, and Heilongjiang, known as Manchuria, in September 1931. Still, the establishment of a puppet government there and finally the creation of the state of Manzhuguo in 1932 was, no doubt, more ominous. So were the armed clashes two years earlier between the Chinese Nineteenth Route Army and Japanese forces in Shanghai's Zhabei district. But it was the outbreak of the Sino-Japanese War, which began with the so-called Marco Polo Bridge Incident in July 1937, spreading to Shanghai one month later that showed the foreign community how vulnerable it in fact was. Neither the International Settlement nor the French Concession was affected, and Zhabei once again bore the brunt of the fighting, as did large areas of Hongkou. The battle in and around Shanghai lasted well into the fall, with a staggering number of civilian and army casualties. Parks Coble writes that "the bloody Battle of Shanghai would become the most intense conflict since Verdun in World War I."[15]

Although calm returned to the city by 1938, dramatic changes were under way as a result of the war. Business was badly affected by the hostilities, and inland shipping to Yangzi ports in particular continued to suffer. The Japanese increasingly asserted themselves by taking over Chinese areas and installing puppet governments; the foreign settlements (now termed *gudao*, or solitary island) were increasingly isolated. Inflation that had been moderate began to soar from mid-1939 on with disastrous impact on the lower classes and especially the poverty-stricken Chinese refugees who had crowded into Shanghai to escape the fighting. In addition to these, the aftermath of the 1937 fighting in Shanghai had created a vast homeless refugee population of the city's residents that taxed existing resources to the limit.[16] A condition of lawlessness gradually spread to many parts of Shanghai, and the city became a crime capital in which racketeering, gambling, the narcotics trade, and prostitution flourished.[17]

It goes without saying that Western businessmen in Shanghai grew increasingly jittery. The temporary boom, starting toward the end of 1938, seemed promising, but was of short duration. The Shanghai Municipal Council was decidedly not coping with the new situation that had arisen as a result of war. Thus, the massive arrival of European refugees from the end of 1938 on must have seemed like the last straw to SMC officials. Moreover, passport controls at the port of entry that had been handled by officials of the Nationalist government had ceased to function with the outbreak of war. Passport control was not assumed by any of the Western powers for fear that the Japanese would want to participate. Therefore, the practice simply lapsed. This has led to the mistaken assumption, stated in most writings on Shanghai and Jewish emigration, that no visas were required. The fact was, however, that the visa requirement became arbitrary; some shipping companies booked passage only if the traveler was in possession of a visa, others did not.

6. A page from *Dos vort* (The word), no. 5, December 6, 1941. Judaica Collection, Harvard College Library (99.774, C4070).

7. Handbill of a performance of *A Better Gentleman*, March 27, 1941. Ralph Harpuder Collection.

8. Roof café "Roy, 1944" (4648/36). Courtesy H. P. Eisfelder Photography Collection (now housed at Yad Vashem Archives, Jerusalem).

The Refugee Flood, December 1938 to September 1939

The refugees that came ashore in December 1938 were blissfully unaware of the profound unease that lurked beneath the surface calm. So were the ones who came thereafter, having narrowly escaped the conflagration that would soon engulf Europe. But the SMC was far from calm when on December 20, 1938, over 500 refugees arrived and when in the next eight months Italian, German, and Japanese ships brought hundreds more. Between July 3 and 31 alone, eight ships docked—four Japanese, one Italian, three German—with 1,315 refugees.[18] In August, eight more ships arrived, among them two from Marseilles bringing the number of refugees now in Shanghai to 17,000. The Shanghai Municipal Police (SMP) apparently dispatched men to the docks to take a headcount, and the *China Press* diligently reported the number of arrivals on each ship. How to handle the new crisis became a major concern in the first half of 1939.

The initial response of the SMC was to prevail on the Jewish organizations in Europe, England, and America to prevent refugees from coming to Shanghai.[19] The council, moreover, let it be known that it would not contribute any funds whatsoever toward maintenance of the refugees, and that the newly created Committee for the Assistance of European Jewish Refugees in Shanghai (CAEJR) would have to assume this responsibility.[20]

Yet, how was Michelle Speelman, the head of the newly created committee and a successful Shanghai businessman and broker, to become suddenly involved in social work? How could his committee possibly find accommodations immediately for thousands of refugees as well as identify ways of feeding them? That the CAEJR managed to do so is much to its credit, despite the delicate situation that developed and that had never before been encountered either by the British or the Jewish community. On the one hand, the British feared that the unchecked influx would lead the Japanese to institute passport control, which, they felt, was damaging to their interests.[21] On the other, the Jewish businessmen, including Speelman, feared loss of respect and prestige in the non-Jewish business community if they were unable to take care of their destitute coreligionists.

The attempt to stop the uncontrolled influx led to the implementa-

tion of the so-called permit system, whereby an entry permit or possession of money was required for landing in Shanghai. The regulation for
Shanghai entry was issued on October 22, 1939, that is, after the start
of World War II in Europe, which in any event prevented German ships
from docking in Shanghai. However, soon after promulgating the regulation, the SMP discovered a serious loophole. Instead of waiting for
a permit, it was easier to procure the necessary funds and depart with
them. As the police report of May 24, 1940, remarked, "Any Tom, Dick,
or Harry can land here provided he has the necessary funds and as many
as a shipload can arrive with each and every steamer."[22] Something
needed to be done, and as a result the revised permit system became ef-
fective July 1, 1940, requiring of arrivals both an entry permit and money.
But this came again too late for the SMC, for in June 1940 Italy joined
Germany in the war, thus eliminating Italian carriers from the refugee
traffic. Although this still left a few other steamers, including Japanese
ones, traveling to Shanghai, the sea route had, for all practical purposes,
ceased by summer of 1940.

Those refugees who arrived in Shanghai before spring and summer
of 1939 had an easier time settling in than later arrivals. They were
taken to flats or rooms rented for them, as related in Annie Witting's
letter of 1939 (below), and were encouraged to embark on an indepen-
dent existence and to earn their livelihood. Many, like the Eisfelder
and Zunterstein families, did just that.[23] Others, who came later,
ended up in shelter facilities, the so-called Heime (homes). These were
large buildings, mostly located in Hongkou, rented or bought by the
CAEJR for the refugees, and quickly reconstructed as dormitory facilities. Although some refugees tried to leave these shelters soon after
arrival, finding rooms or flats to rent, and jobs, however menial, was
often impossibly difficult. Many succumbed to depression and iner-
tia and remained in the shelters. These and the soup kitchens, actually food distribution points connected with them, were financed by
the American Joint Distribution Committee (JDC) through the CAEJR
(or the Speelman Committee, as it came to be known) until the outbreak of the Pacific War. Many refugees, even if they lived in rented
flats, nonetheless obtained a portion of their food from the public
kitchens.

Toward a Life of Culture

It is difficult to imagine what it was like for entire families to leave behind the comforting certainty of familiar surroundings and embark on an exile in unknown parts of the world. Only in retrospect, from a distance of more than half a century, can one say that those who left hearth and home chose life over certain death.

Leaving Austria or Germany in 1938 and 1939, even if the brutality of the new regime was only beginning to be known, was nonetheless a step into the dark unknown. Therefore, one cannot but admire the resilience of the human spirit that allowed these refugees, after what must have been an initial shock, to construct in Hongkou an astonishingly rich cultural life that included publishing, theater, and broadcasting. At the same time, the unique nature of existing Shanghai culture made it possible for these strange newcomers to assert a place for themselves and say "now we [too] are here," as did Egon Varro in his poem "Well, That Too Is Shanghai" (translated below).

With uncommon energy, often great frustration, but also a dose of humor (see Karl Heinz Wolff's poem, "The Diligent Mason," below), the refugees set to renovating, rebuilding, and reconstructing sections of Hongkou that had suffered grievously during the fighting between Chinese and Japanese armed forces in 1937. Not only apartments that could be profitably rented, but renovated coffee houses, new restaurants, and eateries of various kinds—all these sprang up. A coffee house culture was re-created in Hongkou for the benefit of patrons, waiters found employment, and owners acquired income. Entertainers similarly profited from such establishments, and those who could afford it were able to eat real Viennese cakes (!).

Despite numerous problems, German-language theater also flourished when Jewish actors and actresses who had lost their jobs and livelihood early on in Germany and Austria came to Shanghai. However, a proper theater with a large stage did not exist in the city, nor did the actors have funds for costumes and sets. There were also not many scripts and librettos that refugees had brought along and, because audiences were small, plays could not be staged more than once or twice. Variety shows, which could be performed almost anywhere, did not require sets and hardly ever costumes, became favorites, and plays by G. B. Shaw, Molnar,

or Strindberg were also performed on a limited basis. We do not know
how many dramas were actually written in Shanghai, but *Fremde Erde*
(Foreign soil), by Hans Morgenstern (1905–1965) and Mark Siegelberg
(1895–1986), about Shanghai life, is unquestionably a powerful drama
that, if translated, should appeal to audiences even today.[24] Whether
refugee theater had high performance standards or not is a question that
will, no doubt, never be answered. Critics have argued that immigration
cannot be artistically creative because it seeks to conserve those artistic
aspects that it has brought along;[25] that first-rate actresses and actors like
Lily Flohr and Herbert Zernik—to name only two—carried on against
all odds is a credit to their stamina and determination.

The abundance of German Jewish publishing should not come as a
surprise, considering, on the one hand, the determined effort to create
some kind of cultural life, and on the other, the large and small presses
and numerous Chinese- and foreign-language newspapers and journals
already in existence in Shanghai at the time. Established as early as 1939,
German Jewish newspapers and journals came to be about eleven in
number (fig. 9). Among them were two medical journals and the broadly
intellectual monthly, the *Gelbe Post*. Some of these were edited by professional editors, some were short lived, others were not. The publications
frequently changed hands and/or names, and often weeklies became
monthlies. The only paper that survived World War II intact was the
Shanghai Jewish Chronicle, edited by Ossi Lewin.

These papers provided an opportunity for the many professional
journalists who came to Shanghai to continue their careers as well as to
earn small sums of money. Advertisements were an important feature
of the papers, offering services and especially information about stores
where goods might be obtained. Ads were also an important source of
income for the papers. Then there were local news and announcements
of events or performances. Criticism of local Jewry was not often voiced
in the pages of the press, yet Wolfgang Fischer could not refrain from
mentioning that the Russian Jews spent a million on their New Jewish
Club while thousands of refugees went hungry.[26]

Many of the papers featured poetry. These might be pious verses
around holiday time, nostalgic looks backward, or depictions of the local
scene. A satirical touch was not lacking, such as in the poems by Kurt

9. A page from *Die Laterne*, no. 1, June 14, 1941. Reel Y-2003-1854.8. YIVO Institute for Jewish Research.

Lewin or in the poem by Egon Varro that appears here. The prevalence of poetry is not surprising. "Apparently lyrics are the most useful as well as the most intimate means," writes Guy Stern, "for the literary shaping of the exile experience."[27] To this should be added that lyric poems, unlike novels or novellas, are short and more easily published.

Most of the newspapers folded at the outbreak of the Pacific War in December 1941. In fact, journalists and editors were hardest hit by the sudden loss of income. The cessation of funds from the JDC at the same time contributed to a pervasive sense of crisis in the refugee community that had been obvious even earlier, as Shoshana Kahan unhesitatingly confided to her diary entries translated below. Laura L. Margolis was sent by the JDC to Shanghai in May 1941. Rightly or wrongly, she was at once dissatisfied with the way the Speelman Committee was handling financial matters. A trained social worker, Margolis felt the situation in Shanghai left much to be desired, an opinion that some others shared. The problem mainly concerned the Polish refugees, who, some believed, were receiving privileges others did not, or were being neglected in favor of German refugees for certain other services. In a long report dispatched from Kobe, Japan, J. Epstein, an emissary of the Jewish Refugee Relief Organization, wrote that because JDC money is funneled through the Speelman Committee, Polish refugees in Shanghai get even less than the German ones.[28] By summer 1941, the atmosphere of dissension among the various Jewish communities had reached unbearable proportions. Much of it was due to the arrival of the Polish refugees from Japan (to be discussed below) who, like Shoshana Kahan, had taken an instant dislike to Shanghai. They had been treated generously in Kobe, but then they had been the only refugees there.

Much of the acrimony was due to the establishment of a separate relief organization for the Polish refugees in March 1941. Called the Committee for the Assistance of Jewish Refugees from Eastern Europe, known as EastJewCom, its purpose was to handle money allowances for the Polish refugees so that they would not have to live in shelters as the German and Austrian refugees did. The latter justifiably were unable to see why the Polish refugees should receive preferential treatment.

Pearl Harbor and the Pacific War did not put an end to the smoldering antagonism. It would seem that, quite to the contrary, as the military situation grew worse, so did the relationships between the several immigrant factions in Shanghai. Meanwhile, the Japanese, who now occupied the International Settlement as well, gradually created an organizational structure, both Japanese and Jewish, for dealing with the various Jewish groups. Among these on the Jewish side was the Shanghai Ashkenazi Collaborating Relief Association, known as SACRA.[29] Consisting of Russian

Jews, this association was created by the Japanese for the purpose of carrying out directives transmitted to it by the Japanese Bureau of Stateless Refugee Affairs. Its first task, which earned it the bad reputation it would retain throughout the war, was to carry out the aim of the infamous February 18, 1943, Proclamation, whereby the ghetto (or the designated area, as it was called by the Japanese), was officially established.

Despair and outrage greeted the proclamation. It decreed that all stateless persons who had arrived in Shanghai since 1937 must move into the designated area by May 18. People who had managed to establish businesses in the International Settlement or the French Concession, who had rented more desirable flats in better parts of Shanghai, were hardest hit. Not only was the crowding in a small area of Hongkou intolerable, but many lost their source of livelihood. Furthermore, the Japanese required passes to leave the ghetto for work, food shopping, visiting acquaintances, and the like. The person in charge of arbitrarily granting or not granting a pass was Kanoh Ghoya, the self-styled "king of the Jews," who was hated by one and all (figs. 10 and 11), and who is captured in Herbert Zernik's long poem, "A Monkey Turned Human." Before moving on it may be useful, however, to explain how the Polish refugees ended up in Shanghai in 1941.

From Warsaw to Shanghai

It was a motley group of secular and religious Jews, of Zionists and poets, of religious school (yeshiva) students and their rabbis, and of writers that had fled Poland in September 1939. Their odyssey to Shanghai is a story of courage, spiritual strength, and perseverance, for the overland journey that this group embarked on was vastly complicated.

Several groups and some twenty yeshivot[30] from various parts of Poland had fled to Lithuania when the Germans marched into Poland on September 1, 1939. Going mostly to Vilna and Kovno, which had large Jewish communities, they believed Lithuania to be a safe haven, as it was neither conquered by the Germans nor by the Russians, both of whom respected the country's borders for a time. The refugees were indeed hospitably received by Lithuanian Jewry. Many found jobs and were able to support themselves.

Then, in June 1940, a scant nine months after the Germans occupied

Poland, the Red Army marched into Lithuania. When on January 1, 1941, an official decree was promulgated requiring refugees to accept Soviet citizenship or become stateless by January 25, many refugees began to search for ways of leaving. Stateless status, they knew quite well, would land them in Siberia or in one of Russia's Far Eastern provinces. Whereas many refugees did apply for Soviet citizenship, approximately 3,000 to 4,000 of them, for various reasons, desperately attempted to find another solution.[31] Supported by a healthy survival instinct,[32] their search led them first to the Dutch consul, Jan Zwartendijk, from whom they obtained an end-visa for the Dutch colony of Curaçao though, in fact, a visa for Curaçao was not needed.[33] With the end-visa in hand, the refugees next approached the Japanese consul in Kovno, Chiune Sugihara (1900–1986), for a Japan transit visa. This transit visa, in turn, enabled them to obtain Russian exit and transit visas, which they needed for travel to Moscow, where they would board the Trans-Siberian Railway for Vladivostok. The Trans-Siberian journey lasted as long as a week, but the voyage by ship from Vladivostok to Tsuruga on the Japan coast was brief, although it could be highly unpleasant in stormy weather. From Tsuruga, a short railway trip brought the refugees to Kobe, where they remained until mid-1941.

Matters did not always go this smoothly, however. Despite the fact that ships usually sailed from Vladivostok to Tsuruga three times each month,[34] people often got stuck in Vladivostok or, worst of all, were in danger of being sent back. As there was no passenger traffic between Vladivostok and Shanghai, the Shanghai Jewish authorities spared no effort in the attempt to charter ships for the Vladivostok-Shanghai run. Nothing came of it, but the refugees were not sorry to land in Kobe, hoping no doubt to remain there until the end of war. Here is how one of the refugees described his first impression of Kobe:

> A splendid, brightly lit waiting hall. All around hundreds of smiling faces, comfortable faces, soft, loving eyes. Colorful light kimonos are worn by slim, graceful women. There is no pushing, no shoving. . . . Soon they [the Japanese] are ready . . . to help without taking money . . . only to be polite. . . . You feel at once at home . . . in your heart [you feel] good and easy, you believe it will be all right.[35]

Ghoya I.

The former King of Hongkew

No Can

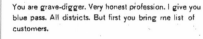

You are grave-digger. Very honest profession. I give you blue pass. All districts. But first you bring me list of customers.

The Dictator plays

If you don't beat proper rythm, Professor, I'll kill you, you dirty swine.

"R" and "L" are becoming a bore

if the Rion starts to Loar.

Either way is wrong

Your English is too good. You better go to America.– No pass. Get out!

Your English is too poor. No English, no business, no pass. Get out!

To Mr. Ghoya
late Japanese official of the
Stateless Refugees' Affairs Bureau
Shanghai- Hongkew
now
????????

Sir,

you called yourself "King of the Jews" assu-
ming your position unshakable. Yet, we knew
better. And in spite of your beating us and
your humilitaing men and women we knew
you pretty well, you little brute - a malicious
frog you were and a ridiculous clown.
We want to smile on you, oh King, and
that's why I pinned you down just as we saw
you and just as we shall remember you - a
maniac, a nightmare but a ridiculous fool
as well.

So long

Shanghai, Sept. 1945

10 and 11. Friedrich Melchior's cartoon about Ghoya together with Melchior's letter. Courtesy Irene Eber Collection, Yad Vashem Archives (078/38).

Unfortunately, the Kobe interlude was of short duration. Less than a year
later, the Japanese began shipping the refugees by stages to Shanghai,
where they were not exactly welcome. Shoshana Kahan's first glimpse
of Shanghai stands in sharp contrast to the reception the refugees had
in Japan.

The secular contingent among the Polish group seemed to be treated
far worse than the religious Jews or even the secular Zionists. Of 300
who arrived August 22, 1941, on the *Asama Maru,* the 140 religious students and their rabbis were at once taken to the Museum Road synagogue for the Friday night (Sabbath) meal with accommodations prepared for them. Twenty-nine Zionists, eventually bound for Palestine,
were taken to the Betar Club in the Jewish Club. But the secular group
had to make do with a rented house where there were neither beds nor
bedding, neither chairs nor tables, neither drinking water nor stoves to

boil water.[36] Despite protests from various official sources in Shanghai over the treatment meted out to this group, private rather than official Jewish assistance, in the form of better accommodations, was offered.[37]

Why nearly 1,000 people were moved at that time from Japan to Shanghai was explained by Koreshige Inuzuka as a legal and economic measure. First, he said, the refugees had been in Japan with only transit visas, which did not enable them to remain there indefinitely. Second was the unfortunate American freezing of Japanese assets so that the JDC, an American organization, could no longer transfer funds to Kobe for the refugees' maintenance.[38] Inuzuka's economic argument makes sense; means had to be found to pay for the refugees' upkeep (there were only twenty-some Jewish families in Kobe), and those means were in Shanghai, not in Kobe. But there is a contradiction here because, at the same time that the Japanese sent more Jews to Shanghai, they were unwilling to admit them to Japanese-controlled Hongkou. Another complication not mentioned by Inuzuka may have been that too many Jews ended up in Japan, leading the Japanese government to fear that a foreign colony was in the making. This may have been the major reason that no more Japanese transit visas were issued, thus closing yet another escape route for Jews fleeing Europe.[39]

An additional problem concerns numbers. How large a group of Jews managed, in fact, to reach Japan? And after some were apparently able to emigrate to other countries, how many were left and ended up in Shanghai? It is doubtful that accurate numbers will be ever available. That Sugihara saved 10,000 by signing this number of transit visas for Japan is surely an exaggeration.[40] According to a report by the Kobe committee of August 1941, 4,413 refugees arrived in Japan between July 1, 1940, and June 1, 1941. Of these, 3,092 departed for various destinations and 1,321 remained in Japan.[41] We can assume that these figures are reasonably accurate, and it makes sense to assume from available newspaper notices that a little over 1,000 Polish refugees (with probably a number of Lithuanians among them) ended up in Shanghai.

Considering their small numbers and their repeated dislocation, as well as their relative alienation in Shanghai from the Central European refugees, the fact that they, too, attempted to create a semblance of cultural life is remarkable. The arrival of several Jewish-Polish actors in 1941, for example, brought life to the Yiddish stage in Shanghai, at least for a time, with the performance of several well-known plays. The problems encountered by the German-language theater were, however, also encountered by the Yiddish theater. The lack of money for costumes and settings, and of time for rehearsals when actors had to hold down jobs to earn a living, was not conducive to a flourishing Yiddish theater. Variety shows and Yiddish song evenings made fewer demands on performers. Nonetheless, a performance of the perennially popular play *Der dibek* (The dybbuk) took place in November 1941, and *Mirele Efros*, with Shoshana Kahan, was performed February 1942.[42]

The other area in which Yiddish speakers could be active was publishing. To be sure, most if not all papers and journals published in Yiddish were short lived and ceased in 1942. Still, it is remarkable that the incentive to bring out a paper was not lacking. Of major importance was the Yiddish page, *Undzer lebn* (Our life), which appeared in the Russian paper *Nasha Zhizn*. In addition, there were five other papers, two of these religious, *Dos vort* (The word) and *Di yidishe shtime fun vaytn mizrekh* (The Jewish voice from the Far East), published by Agudas Yisroel. Secular papers like *Yedies* (News), or *In veg* (On the way) are interesting for their literary tendencies and provided an opportunity for writers to make themselves heard.

For all the stateless refugees, no matter what their countries of origin, the war years were difficult, made worse by their crowding into Hongkou. The two-and-a-half years from February 1943 to August 1945, when the JDC representatives, Laura Margolis and Manuel Siegel, were interned, were the hardest. During that time, the refugees were entirely dependent on SACRA and the several committees that were created by the Japanese for managing refugee affairs. A lengthy report by Manuel Siegel after the war characterized refugee life as rife with personal animosities, suspicions, hostility, and selfishness. A major reason why the refugees turned on one another and especially on the committees, whom they completely distrusted, was that, aside from issuing passes, the Japanese interfered very little directly in refugee affairs. Thus the refugees did not vent their wrath on the occupier.[43] Indeed, "the refugee Jews, while naturally anti-Nazi, were not particularly hostile to the Japanese—to whom many of them felt gratitude for affording them an escape hatch from Nazi Europe," writes Bernard Wasserstein.[44] And even when the large majority of refugees were segregated in the Hongkou district, they tended to blame the Germans for having instigated this. Herbert Zernik's satire about the universally hated Ghoya was written, it should be noted, after the war and attacks a specific man. It is not directed against the Japanese occupation.

Resentment was especially directed against the Shanghai Jewish Joint Distribution Committee, established after the demise of the Speelman Committee and headed by C. Brahn. Brahn was characterized by Siegel as an eccentric man, who was abusive and high-handed and who had no regard for decisions reached in the committee, a view shared by most refugees. He was closely associated with powerful Japanese men, and people generally feared him.[45] Cut off from all contact with their families in Europe, the refugees had no idea what the fate of their loved ones had been during the war years. Even at war's end in 1945, the terrible story of suffering and death came to be known only gradually. And while their families were never far from their minds, the refugees' daily struggle and hardships in Shanghai took their toll.

Although the end of war was greeted with much relief by the refugees, new problems were at once apparent. Some young people managed to land jobs with the Americans, hoping by such means to obtain the much-coveted visa to the United States. Others thought it best to go "home" to Germany or Austria, even though reports of the widespread destruction were reaching Shanghai. Still others thought that perhaps remaining in Shanghai and starting a business was not a bad option. In 1945, in any event, possibilities for departing from Shanghai were practically nonexistent. Meanwhile, funds were needed for providing continued relief for thousands of people.

When civil war began to engulf China in 1946, leaving Shanghai became a priority for the refugees. Gradually, they departed to countries that would have them: Australia, Canada, the United States, and, after 1948, the newly established state of Israel. They carried with them memories that for children and teenagers were somehow gilded, filled with wonder, while their parents would remember the hardships of those Shanghai years, the culture shock that greeted them upon arrival. The children of yesterday are a little older now, but they still meet every few years at "rickshaw reunions" in various parts of the world and talk about times gone by. The diarist, the inspired letter writer, are all but forgotten, and not many remember the poets who in lonely hours wrote moving verses about Shanghai and their fate in that city. Over the years the winds of history covered their verses with sand.[46]

Chinese and Jews and Literary Encounters

A question that still demands even a brief answer is how much these German- or Yiddish-speaking writers and poets might have known about China. What images might they have had of the large metropolis Shanghai?

Literature about China and translations from Chinese had been accumulating in German since the nineteenth century, if not earlier. Nationalism, the occupation of Jiaozhou Bay by Germany in 1897, and the dispatch of German missionaries stimulated interest in that faraway empire. Literature and philosophy were a major concern, and China's classical literature found ready translators. Yet China for the most part was the "Other," the counter-world to the German *Zeitgeist*.[47] Notwithstanding the inevitable distortions, a German reader could read about China in popular novels like Alfred Döblin's 1917 *Die drei Sprünge des Wang-lun* (Wang-lun's three leaps), for example, and from newspapers he might learn something about the troubling events in China. In short, without too much effort, the German reader could learn some facts about the country, its people, and its culture.

The Yiddish reader similarly need not have been entirely uninformed. Inexpensive books about Chinese history, philosophy, and literature were available. There was, for example, a book about Confucius and another about Laozi; the former was published in Warsaw in a well-known series about important world figures, and the latter in Berlin.[48] The multivolume work *Di velt geshikhte* (World history), by Jacob Dinezohn, opens with a thirty-nine-page chapter about Chinese history, and Nahum Bomse (1906–1954) published a book of translations of poems by the Tang dynasty poet Li Bai.[49] Books were not the only source of information; Yiddish newspapers also carried news about China, including Shanghai.

Thus the popular and widely read paper, *Der moment*, established in

1913, printed the far-flung journeys to Japan and China in 1927 of Peretz Hirshbein (1880–1948).[50] *Haynt* (Today) was another widely read daily, and in its pages a reader could find articles on current events in China, and especially the problems that followed the outbreak of the Sino-Japanese War in July 1937.[51] Such is the barest outline of what a Yiddish reader had available. It must not be assumed, however, that this interest was one-sided. Chinese readers, too, were exposed to aspects of Yiddish literature, and chapters from Jewish history were publicized in several periodicals.[52] These intercultural intellectual interests of peoples remote and culturally distant from one another are very interesting and certainly deserve further exploration.

The selections of poetry and prose translated into English in these pages are the work of refugees and appeared for the most part in Yiddish and German Shanghai newspapers. I succumbed to the temptation of adding one Polish poem, which appeared in the Polish paper published in Shanghai and adds still one other dimension to the refugee experience. More of some truly exceptional pieces are contained in other Shanghai papers that, all but forgotten, are gathering dust in various archives on several continents. At least one poem has appeared in a book,[53] and Shoshana Kahan's diary, too, was published as a book. Yehoshua Rapoport's important diary, on the other hand, remains in manuscript form. Not all the poems were written by poets; some were penned by actors, like "A Monkey Turned Human" by Herbert Zernik. Two of the poems included here, and most likely never published, are in the Shanghai Municipal Police Files, submitted apparently to the censor as part of materials for a variety show. Unfortunately, very few diaries have survived the ravages of time, and even fewer collections of letters. Shoshana Kahan's diary is unique, not only because it is a published diary, but also because it records a woman's perception, and women's voices are notably scarce in Shanghai writing. Equally unique are the excellent letters by Annie Witting that relay first impressions of life in Shanghai and describe the ingenious ways in which these middle-class women made a living.

The translations are arranged chronologically from 1937 to 1947, except for the first poem by Meylekh Ravitch, which is from 1935, and the diary selections, which are from several periods as well as from the end of war. The chronological arrangement often reveals more clearly the event the poem is a response to. With few exceptions, therefore, the poems do not deal with timeless themes, or explore the poet's inner life. They should be considered part of exile literature and record the poets' shock, amazement, or surprise at situations he or she finds unusual in this unique city.

* MEYLEKH RAVITCH *

(ZEKHARIA KHONE BERGNER, 1893–1976)[54]

Meylekh Ravitch (fig. 12) was born in the small Polish town of Radimno, not far from Przemyśl. He was educated by private teachers and in 1910 began working in a bank, first in Lvov, then in 1912 in Vienna. Like most other poets, he began writing poetry at an early age; in his late teens he became a vegetarian, something quite unusual at the time. After World War I, in 1921, he moved to Warsaw with his wife and two young children. In Warsaw he contributed significantly to the growth and development of modern Yiddish poetry; he was secretary of the Yiddish Writers and Journalists' Association, and founder as well as secretary of the Yiddish Pen section. But Ravitch was also an inveterate traveler who claimed to have visited forty-four countries by the time he was forty years old. He began his China journey by going first to London and from there, in January 1935, to Moscow, from where he traveled on the Trans-Siberian railway to the Manchurian border and then to Harbin. In China he visited major cities: Beijing, Tianjin, Guangzhou (Canton), and Shanghai. He did not return to Poland, but traveled on to Australia. There he wrote poems about each of the cities he had visited in China in addition to the Trans-Siberian journey and the Yangzi River. All of these are included in his *Kontinentn un okeanen*[55] (Continents and oceans), from which this poem is translated.

∾

12. Meylekh Ravitch. From an article in English titled "Ort-Oze Combat Economic Life in Europe: Interview with Mr. Melech Ravitsh" in "Israel's Messenger," Vol. 32, May 3, 1935, p. 23.

A RICKSHAW COOLIE DIES ON A
SHANGHAI DAWN (1937)

Wearily morning drags into Shanghai,
In long rows of rickshaws men doze.
Sitting all night outside they chew empty-mouthed,
Pale clouds east, west a blue sky.

Someone cries. Somewhere toward the front of the long row.
"Who weeps among us?" each man asks the other.
"Chen Zungui. Why? A serious matter. A hurt foot.
What else?" He is dying, felled by a fever's blow.

Chen runs from the row. "Where to? You'll lose your turn.
Has the devil caught you?"
Chen runs, rickshaw dancing behind.
A Buddhist temple. He bends down, removes the sandal-like shoe.

"Open up, sleepy horse! For my last
three coppers get up and open!"
Before he expires Chen Zungui must
Meet Buddha face to face.

The rusty keys turn
A wooden bolt groans.
Chen Zungui opens the gate, yawning
Buddha awakens. He smiles. The flame dances in an urn.

"Here I am, Buddha, as I walk and stand,
A nail smolders in my foot, in my belly hunger smolders.
Listen to me, look, I prepared
three brown coppers in my black hand.

I'm still Chen Zungui—but soon it will end—
I'm still one of five hundred million.
From you I want nothing, not even an easy death.
I only want to remind you of this transient.

Spit woodenly on me, on Chen Zungui, worse than a dog,
In my face that under a roof never had lain.
I don't even know it, never seen it in a mirror,
Only in puddles, in water from rain.

Even greater the hunger in Jiangsu province.
My wife and children wither away sickly.
Three coppers for three lives, take it for them
And let them be buried ever more quickly.

I want Nirvana. I, worse than a stray,
Now with torn foot from rusty iron,
With fever I burn, yet not a one
will even shoot me compassionately.

But if Chen Zungui a dog had been,
With water his wound would be bathed.
A bone to chew would be readied for him,
And a mercy killing would not be a sin.

Don't smile, Buddha, wake up, Chen has no wealth.
He can't give three coppers for nought in return.
Chen wants to pay and finish, he's earned it.
Open your wooden hand, Chen wants to give you his life, his health."

Buddha hears, extends his hand, smiles again,
Chen Zungui stretches, smiles at Buddha,
On his face a first and last smile.
A face that was always mirrored in puddles of rain.

Chen Wushen, the servant, angrily comes.
He takes the coppers from the crooked hand.
Later he drags the dead man by the healthy foot.
"Where to put him?" He raises his shoulders and hums.

Although Meylekh Ravitch was not a refugee like the others in this collection, he could not be omitted. Ravitch was in Shanghai only a short time, all of six weeks in 1935. Unlike the refugees who arrived six years later, he had visas for elsewhere and money that would take him anywhere in the world. Yet the compassion for the suffering of a fellow human being and anger at an indifferent world—indeed, we might call this the spirit of humanism—Ravitch had in common with other poets in these pages. In the travelogue where Ravitch recorded his China impressions, the Shanghai section is the longest and takes up fourteen pages in all.[56] Rickshaw pullers, suffering "hell on earth in Shanghai," the poorest of the poor, especially engaged his attention. He recorded his indignation at their fate in a vignette about a rickshaw man who has stepped on a piece of glass, but continues to run while the glass cuts deeper and deeper into his foot.[57] No doubt, the notation in the travelogue is the basis of this poem, which he wrote after his arrival in Melbourne. In it he expressed not only his moral indignation, but he also indicates the futility of religious faith. For a moment, the injured man thinks the wooden idol is alive, but lest we, the readers, also succumb to the illusion, Ravitch tells us in the last verse that the temple servant takes the money and drags the dead man away.

The story that Ravitch tells in this poem about one rickshaw man is not the only story for which he chose the poetic form. Story poems are also told about Beijing, Harbin, and Canton (Guangzhou). The poet takes one scene or one event he has seen and makes of it a story as seen through eyes of one who hails from elsewhere. Thus, in this poem about Shanghai, as well as the others he wrote, Ravitch creates a wonderful intercultural fusion, seemingly without effort, capturing imaginatively and in few words the two worlds.

ANNIE F. WITTING *

(ANNE FELICITAS WITTING, Born Wilhelm, 1904–1971)[58]
The Wilhelm family was originally from Poznan, Poland, and lived in
Berlin beginning in 1922. Annie Witting (fig. 13) was married in 1927,
after having worked briefly in a bookstore, but she seems not to have had
any business experience, which she exhibited so markedly in Shanghai.
She was in her mid-thirties when she wrote the letters included here.
Peter Witting, Annie's son, writes that "she kept carbon copies of all the

letters she had written and I suspect that
she also retyped some of the letters."
Growing up in an upper-middle-class
household and having lived a very shel-
tered life, nothing prepared her for the
Shanghai experience. The Wittings lived
in Shanghai for eight years, leaving for
Australia in 1947.

13. Photograph of Annie F. Witting (February
1939). By permission of H. P. Witting.

LETTER (July 1939)

To all my dear friends:
We are already in our new homeland for four weeks and are able to view
from a greater distance all the new things that are strange for Europeans. I am able to report to you, therefore. But I would like to know first
if you have received the detailed account that I wrote on board ship and
mailed from Singapore or Hong Kong.

We reached Shanghai on June 4, at approximately 1 o'clock. After several hours spent on passport and customs formalities, we were taken by
truck at 4 o'clock in the afternoon together with other immigrants from

the ship to one of the refugee shelters [Heime]. We were living thirty-four people to a room, women, men, and children together. From a European perspective, bathroom facilities are indescribably bad. We had to wait in long lines for meals and, despite the bad weather, had to walk a quarter of an hour to get to the place. For breakfast we received tea in enamel cups and dry bread; for lunch [the main meal] a casserole dish; for dinner tea, dry bread, and two eggs or two bananas. This is the reality of shelter life. Every shelter inhabitant must also work from time to time in the kitchen or in the rooms, which is something I have also done. But it is not objectionable; to work a little is not bad; however, the limited horizon of most of the people in the shelters and the entire immigrant environment is depressing. Thanks to the generosity of my brother we had to endure this for only two days and were then able to search for a room of our own. Fortunately, we found one in the house of a Viennese architect couple. We have a large room with a balcony, a garden, telephone, running warm and cold water, bathroom including toilet—none of which is easily come by. Aside from us, there are fifteen other immigrants in this house, among them a dentist from Berlin. . . .

The population of Shanghai is 4½ million; of these, only 50,000 are Europeans, a sign that the climate is quite unhealthy. It is always humid, both in warm and in cold weather. At night, thank heaven, it is cooler, which is not the case in India, for example. Many precautionary measures are: only to drink boiled water; never to walk outside without sunglasses because of the danger of sunstroke; to eat only boiled fruit; not to walk barefoot on the floor because of the danger of Hong Kong foot infection [presumably a fungal infection—ed.]. This is a bad skin disease, very difficult to cure. Moreover, the danger of epidemic diseases is great. On the ship we were all immunized against cholera, smallpox, typhus, and typhoid. But here we had to do it a second time, and must repeat it four times a year. One must never go to sleep without a mosquito net and, in addition, one must light an aromatic candle as an additional preventive measure. I have now told you so much about China's drawbacks, especially about the many cautionary measures to be observed each day, so that you, my dear friends, will surely feel sorry for the Europeans who are forced to live here. Most certainly this was not my intention. I only wanted to tell you about life in Asia without rose-colored glasses.

Shanghai is a world-famous port city and most interesting. Immigrants who have not yet found a job live mostly in the Japanese area of Hongkou. But here, there are also very many German stores and enterprises established by immigrants. In short, it is like a ghetto with the difference that in between many Chinese and Japanese are also settled. Commercial life takes place in the city, the so-called International Settlement. But it would be wrong to think of the International Settlement as only a European area. On the contrary, many Chinese live there, and, as can be gathered from the population statistics, Chinese are in fact in the majority.

Transportation facilities are much more diverse than in Berlin: elegant cars, rickshaws, buses, streetcars, and the like. Distances are enormous. Shortly after our arrival, we bought a map in order to orient ourselves more rapidly. Now we feel altogether like natives and take pride in helping other immigrants find their way. But we commiserate with the poorest among them, who are completely dependent on the support of the [Speelman] committee. Yet, it is a gigantic undertaking, if one considers how much the committee accomplishes. Thousands of immigrants are housed and fed. By the end of the year 20,000 immigrants are expected. That is, by then 20,000 immigrants will be here, and the majority will be given room and board by the committee. All things considered, what the committee offers each individual is enormously generous. The immigrants only lack money, and many do not even have sufficient carfare to go to the city and look for a job.

We have already made excellent connections; we were invited by a British university professor and we also visited several European homes. Connections are very important here, much more important than in Europe. Our export scheme is beginning to take shape. . . . On the whole, life in Shanghai is not too expensive. Rents, however, are exorbitant. A two-room flat can be had for 160 Reichsmark and a furnished room costs 50 to 60 Rm. Food is relatively inexpensive, and cheapest of all is the laundry. A linen jacket, laundered and ironed, costs 4 Pfennig, German money. Of course, wages are equally low. You will readily understand that it is not easy to compete with a Chinese worker. In order to succeed here a person must be a trained professional.

Rain in Shanghai is comparable to a cloudburst in Europe. A person needs high rubber boots to walk in the street. Until December the climate is reasonably pleasant, we are told, like spring in Europe. We have a nice circle of acquaintances, partly friends from the ship who, like us, want to leave behind the immigrant status and not drown in it, as so many seem to. They don't have a goal and have no aspirations to achieve anything. They are satisfied with a roof over their head, a check each month from relatives, and an affordable boy and amah [cleaning and all-around-man and nurse maid—ed.]. We pity them! As for ourselves, we are happy to be free human beings again and to have the possibility of creating an existence for ourselves. Although we left with heavy heart, we don't ever want to return. We have lost too much there and have suffered too much.

We have already requested that the American consulate in Berlin send our papers to the Shanghai consulate. Perhaps we will have the opportunity in another year to leave for the United States. The climate is unhealthy here, and the danger of epidemics is ever present.

We want to send the children to an English school. Because of the heat, vacation time lasts until September. The children are feeling very well, especially because of our beautiful garden. Marion already communicates splendidly with our boy, whom we share with the other tenants for three Shanghai dollars each month. We eat the main meal at noon out for the time being, and I prepare breakfast and a light supper. Our possessions have not arrived yet. Since the rate was cheaper, we sent them via Hamburg and South Africa. I find that a wardrobe-trunk and sleeping bag are preeminently practical, and I strongly recommend taking these along.

We even went out a few times already to a roof garden where there is dancing and which is especially frequented by Englishmen and Americans. And how are you doing? Here I have written so much about us and have not even asked how you all have been. Please write to us very soon.

My best regards,
Annie Witting

Annie Witting's letters are addressed to family and friends; she probably attached brief personal notes to them. They are remarkable for several reasons. She was an astute observer and knew how to record her observations. It is significant that she never used the word "refugee" (Flüchtling), but consistently referred to the newcomers as immigrants (Emigranten). To be sure, "immigrant" was preferred by most of the newcomers, yet it also indicates that she did not identify herself as a victim, an expellee, but as one who hoped to begin a new life in a new place. Still, she had no illusions. Her reports about Shanghai, the unhealthy climate, the care one must take not to fall ill, the difficult living conditions, all this she recounted without embellishment. Above all, Witting seemed to indicate, a person must not succumb to misfortune, but must continue to have goals and, as we will see in a subsequent letter, strive to improve the present. Whereas others consistently criticized and found faults with the Speelman Committee, Annie Witting also saw the gigantic task these businessmen had taken on. They were not trained social workers, but knowing that they had no choice but see to the minimal needs of the newcomers, they tried to do their best. With rare perception, Witting gave them credit for making sure that everyone had a place to live and that no one starved.

* ALFRED FRIEDLAENDER *

(?–?)

All that is known of Alfred Friedlaender is that he was an engineer by profession. The poem translated below was written to commemorate a Hanukah celebration, December 6, 1939, at 992 Tongshan Road in Shanghai. It was recited that evening by Mrs. Illy Hirshensohn, the host of the evening, as part of the evening's entertainment.

PROLOGUE (1939)[59]

The home of Crabs reached a resolve
That all its comrades must observe
To celebrate the festival
of Hanukah without reserve.
A happy ev'ning for one's mood
And for the stomach pleasant food.

Let's glance at our master now,
He's not bad looking for a Crab.
His English is not elegant,
He doesn't have the gift of gab,
But in Chinese he makes much sense
And with his boy he is great friends.

Perform she must, our Mrs. Crab,
She swells and puffs with pride
As songs and whistles
issue forth by day as well as night.
Even a yodel's heard at times,
Though sounding Jewish when it rhymes.

Daughter Stella's diligent,
Standing at the kitchen range,
She is cooking, frying, baking,
Many think it rather strange.

Mouths are Dr. Rubinstein's specialty,
He was a dentist not so long ago.
But now he only thinks about himself,
Still, when he fights it is with much gusto.

Once Mr. Burgheim looked the other way.
A loudspeaker he swallowed accidentally.
Now when he whispers, though without intent,
His voice booms forth exponentially.

Like twins the couple Hirshensohn,
Year in year out their voices never raise,
Their marriage's firm, they love each other
Because the wife commands and he obeys.

Father Witting, this ill-disposed man,
Drinks only what disgusts the rest.
We hope this custom he'll forswear,
Here's to good health and all the best.

Mother Witting's at the stove and phone,
Running a thriving export enterprise.
Frenchtown is were she feels at home,
But Tongshan Road's the place to fraternize.

They call her Marion, Merson, Marianderl,
We're not really pleased the way she is.
And only hope that our proclamation here
Will make her good like us and submissive.

Peter no doubt will be an engineer,
He putters and fusses, there's none to hire,

To make light in dark corners,
As he with batteries and wire.

Family Gelb has drawn a red line,
In their battle with the mice population.
Not a mouse would ever dare cross it,
Thus we bring the Gelbs an ovation.

The poet's nephew is misbegotten,
In our house he's an infrequent guest.
Between two at night and noon at twelve,
One finds him sleeping and at rest.

Losses too we must lament,
Rising from our seats,
We speak in our eulogy
Of Macky's and Lumpi's lives content.
These noble dogs
Died noble deaths
So that in heaven's canine choir
They always bark and never tire.

Devoutly silent we commence,
To happily conclude this meeting
With Sherry, our skillful guardian,
Who has for food a noisy greeting.
Then there is Mushi, cat insatiable,
Twelve kittens grow in her ample belly.
Not to forget our boy so capable,
A son of heaven he's no doubt,
We're satisfied without complaint,
For he unfailingly does us proud.

The poet's modest, dislikes hoopla,
His only plea to understand his muse.
He wishes all a pleasant Hanukah
And naught but good for Jews.

⊗

"Prologue," though the effort of an amateur, is evocative and gently satirical, bringing humor to what was surely not an easy situation. At the
time, fifteen people lived in the seven-room house owned by Sigmund
and Adele Krebs (*Krebs* is German for "crab," hence the "Crabs" in
the early stanzas). But, as Peter Witting informed me, this number in-
creased to twenty-three in nine rooms when, after February 1943, stateless refugees had to move into Hongkou. Clearly indicated in the poem
are the differences among the inhabitants of this building. Ordinar-
ily, this group of people would have had little if anything in common,
and they certainly would not have lived in such close proximity to one
another.

But these were not normal times, war had broken out in Europe,
loved ones had been left behind, and life was far from simple in Shanghai. Hongkou was not yet as crowded as it would become three years
later, but even in 1939 the refugees required a large degree of tolerance
for one another in order to manage. Perhaps the poet exaggerated certain characteristics, Burgheim's booming voice, for example, or the late
hours kept by the poet's nephew; still some of the people's habits must
have been annoying. The poem conveys, even if jokingly, the crowded
conditions these upper-middle-class refugees found themselves in, the
adjustments they had to make from the comfortable circumstances of
their previous existence.

The Hongkou house no longer stands, as Peter Witting discovered in
April 2006, demolished due to the widening of Dalian Road. However,
this poem, composed as light entertainment for a small and ill-assorted
circle of housemates, stands as an abiding monument and witness to
the Shanghai refugees' resilience. Alfred Friedlaender's voice may be
that of an amateur, but it is a voice well worth listening to.

✳ *EGON VARRO* ✳

(1918–1975)[60]
Varro wrote for various newspapers while in Shanghai, founded his own
short-lived paper, *Der Queerschnitt,* in July 1939, and also worked for
the British Information Service. He managed to leave Shanghai in 1941
with a group of refugees bound for Australia, where he joined the British
army. He apparently wrote for German papers after World War II and
participated in German radio broadcasts in addition to publishing in
Australian journals.[61]

WELL, THAT TOO IS SHANGHAI (1939)[62]

Descending at last from the ship,
one is about to think
of nothing, even the trip,
perhaps a little about money.
But suddenly one must be gone

because here come on the run
with our luggage
three hundred coolies
who sing, grunt, snort, and raise a cry.
Well, that too is Shanghai.

At the Bund they ask: "parlez-vous
Français?"
Around the corner a Berliner yells:
"Ach nee!"
The press greets us: "How do
you do?"
Uncomprehending, the coolies
look too.

In the bus, that's bursting full,
a voice is heard; "hablo español?"
At last come three Viennese.
They want to know from an Italianese
if the Chinese post office is nearby.
Well, that too is Shanghai.

A bus to Hongkou's convenient transport,
and if it's full one can walk
or try a rickshaw.
If the route you know,
the price is low,
but if politely you ask
what may be the fare,
the answer is:
"One dollar from here to there."

A blessing indeed
instead of wealth and gain,
we have in this city several hours of rain.
No strangers we to the unexpected,
it's no surprise,
when even umbrellas fly.
Well, that too is Shanghai.

In Europe and here
we do admit
that man is a creature of habit.
Even if Babylonian babble informs
about dollar exchange, lira and pound,
about unhealthy small pox,
skyscrapers, coolies, and money found,
Nanking Road and shark teeth.

A Shanghai man is not frightened by these
because one must live and has duties.
Even if people who dwell

in small towns say
that effort does not pay,
in a hundred years everything's gone by,
but now we are here:
And this too is Shanghai!

At first glance, we might be tempted to dismiss this poem as a typical expression of Western superiority, ridiculing the "quaint" Chinese. Upon closer scrutiny, however, Varro's poem can be seen as an excellent example of exile literature. The twenty-one-year-old man suddenly finds himself in a cosmopolitan city, such as he has never seen before, surrounded by people from various parts of the world, speaking different languages; the Chinese, whose land after all this is, all seem to be lowly laborers, coolies. His response is altogether unlike the response of some of the Polish-Jewish writers who registered their moral outrage at the condition of the Chinese in this city of great wealth and abject poverty. Instead, Varro chose parody, composing a satirical poem that reveals his own reaction to the languages, the overloaded buses, the incessant rain, the currency and the city's lack thereof. Satirizing his own exiled condition may be considered a defense, "a weapon against the despoilers of tradition at home, and at the same time a self-corrective."[63] The last six lines are, therefore, poignant: the struggle may be futile, yet the young man asserts, "now we are here," as much a part of the roiling international landscape of the city as any ethnic or religious group or nationality.

* W. Y. TONN *

(WILLY TONN, 1902–1957)
Without question, Willy Tonn was one of the most remarkable emigrés ever to come to China in this period. Although he was part of the refugee community and worked among them, he was not really a refugee and did not consider himself as such. He was the son of an affluent German-Jewish family and had studied Asian languages, including Chinese, in Berlin. Tonn arrived in Shanghai in April 1939, "driven by a longing for the East," as he put it.[64] No one did more while in Shanghai to interpret China and Chinese ways to the refugees, both by means of his many articles in the local press and by means of his famous Asia Seminar. The latter was organized in 1943 and continued until 1948. On and off, the seminar had about thirty lecturers who taught languages, including special courses in Chinese for physicians and lawyers, as well as Chinese philosophy and science. Tonn moved to Israel in 1949.[65]

PECULIAR SHANGHAI (1940)[66]

A Holy Tooth

One day I bit into an unpeeled rice kernel and, when I removed it, out came the crown of one of my teeth. Only the shabby root remained. With a bitter heart, I went to the dentist, asking him to pull the stump. In accordance with his nature and in contrast to mine, the dentist was very cheerful, which added considerably to my bad humor. Carelessly, he almost threw my stump into the garbage. It belonged to me, after all, and I had paid five dollars for its removal. Fortunately, he did not succeed.

Next I went to the shop of an old Shanghailander couple from Belgium in order to buy a muffler for the coming winter. After the purchase, they inquired with concern why my cheek was swollen, whereupon I told them about my mishap with the tooth.

Perfectly seriously, and despite my resistance, the couple actually wanted to buy the stump. The negotiations took a full hour, during which

I also mentioned that it was unwise to relinquish a part of one's body because it could be misused for magical purposes. It was, all considered, a
holy relic like the Buddha's tooth in the famous Kandy Temple in Ceylon.
To pay only five dollars for such a precious tooth [as the couple offered]
was not enough. Compared to hair or fingernails a tooth cannot grow
again. Nothing helped; I had to yield the stump for ten dollars.

I should mention that prior to emigrating from Berlin an energetic
antiquities dealer bought one of my fingernails, measuring five centime-
ters, for twenty-five Reichsmark. I had placed the nail in a glass box on
pink cotton and said it was a holy Buddhist relic.

Heavenly Police

Everyone has experiences with Chinese employees. I have mine with my
amah [housekeeper] who is twenty-six years old and the mother of three
children. She's been with me more than a year; she tidies up, does laundry, shops, and also cooks Chinese dishes. God and a little "squeeze"
make working for me worthwhile for her. I live in a house where there
are only Chinese tenants. I gained this privilege [to be among Chinese
tenants] in exchange for the customary *bubao* [Chinese security], several
other ceremonies, lowering of the rent, and suitable classical sayings.

The house is, of course, crowded: there are five more amahs and an
aged "boy" [handyman]. As there is much laundry and general confu-
sion, things get stolen on and off, small items like handkerchiefs that,
upon complaint, usually reappear. One day a tremendous commotion
was again heard and my amah tearfully ran into my room, crying "a
qiangdao [robber] stole *shi kuaiqian* [ten dollars] and a new *yishang*
[dress]." Well, I am used to sorrow and grief and reacted only half-
heartedly to my amah, whose pretty name is Ah Shila, deciding that she
merely wanted to extract some money from me to send to her husband.
Still, moved by compassion, I suggested she go to the Municipal Police
station, taking along my visiting card, the five other amahs, and the
"boy," to lodge a complaint.

One and all in the startled house were wildly enthusiastic over the
waiguoren's [foreigner's] proposal, except the one concerned. . . . Re-
membering the old adage not to have traffic with authority while alive
and after death not with hell (as we say: don't go to your sovereign if he

doesn't call you), the amah pleaded with me not to send her to the police. The other amahs (she argued) had more money and would be, therefore, considered in the right. It seemed highly unlikely to her, and there was no way I could assure her, that filing a complaint would cost no money and that the officials would not demand any. The popular notion that whoever pays more is more in the right was too deeply ingrained.

As a result of her refusal, an ancient custom was reenacted. A table was placed in the middle of the lane together with an incense cauldron and approximately fifty burning incense sticks. All six amahs and the "boy" congregated around the table and were immediately surrounded by several hundred Chinese watching from balconies and roof gardens of the adjoining houses. Then the performance began. My amah was first. She bowed, knelt in front of the table and prayed in ringing tones and with raised arms to the gods. She related the story of the theft, lamented over her hard lot, pleading with the gods to help her and punish the evildoers. Thereafter each amah had to kneel, say her prayer, protest her innocence, call endless misfortunes on her head if she told a lie, and plead for finding the thief and the stolen goods. The "boy" performed the ceremony last. My amah once more knelt, repeated her accusations and her prayer, and again called on the gods to vent their anger on the miscreants.

It was interesting that no one uttered a suspicion or accusation against those present so that none would lose face. Next morning, amazingly, Ah Shila showed me the dress and money she had found on her bed upon waking. Sometimes, it would seem, the gods are more efficient than the police.

The two vignettes translated above present a slice of Shanghai life. In the first, the author laughs at his own deviousness, having once cheated a Berlin antiquarian. He is, he insinuates, as good at the game of passing off a worthless tooth as a relic, and as adept at bargaining as any Chinese.

But should we suspect the second vignette of Orientalism? Is Tonn romanticizing Chinese ways? On closer examination, this does not seem to be the case. Theft was an everyday occurrence in Shanghai life at the time, and Tonn, therefore, does not tell the reader anything new. What is new is his detailed description of a ritual in which local deities are invoked to intervene. The amah firmly believes in their efficacy, but the thief believes similarly in the gods' ability to punish. By telling this little story, Tonn did not intend to show "those quaint Chinese." Rather, I suspect his aim was to explain the extent to which ceremony and ritual have a place in everyday Chinese life.

* ANNIE F. WITTING *

LETTER (Shanghai, January 4, 1940)[67]

To all my dear friends!

Now it is already 1940. You are in Europe, we are in our new homeland in China. . . . But first of all, I send you my heartfelt wishes for health and realization of all your wishes and hopes for the future.

You think most likely that the Wittings have forgotten you, but that is not the case. Unfortunately, we have lived through some difficult times. First, I had tropical dysentery for six weeks, and then my husband came down with an especially severe case for fourteen weeks. As a result of the dysentery, he developed inflammation of the heart. He was in the English hospital for four weeks and at home the rest of the time. The physician came every day for twelve weeks. We had a very capable Berlin physician who [has lived here for] eight years and is especially adept at dealing with cases of exhaustion after tropical diseases. Every day, I had to buy quantities of medicines, and a most careful diet had to be maintained, etc. In addition, especially good nursing care was required, which was very expensive. These were very difficult weeks for us that we have, however, thank heaven, overcome. My husband has recovered somewhat, even if not 100 percent. He still has to be very careful. Heart inflammation is not quickly cured, and he has lost forty pounds that he must gain back.

Aside from nursing my husband, I also had to shoulder responsibility for my family and above all for the finances. On the one hand, we had the support of my brother; on the other, I began several export enterprises (undergarments, pig intestines, etc.). I also sold the crystal that we did not need, and that fetches a good price here. With the money, I bought U.S. dollars when the dollar was low and sold when it was high. In these transactions, I earned quite a bit. Of course, for such ventures, I only used money I could do without and therefore was able to wait for a favorable exchange. I also sold sport coats that I had brought to Shanghai from a German sport clothes company. . . . The Chinese are adept at copying and, under the supervision of a European cutter, are producing them now. The British "Popeline" has been similarly successful; it is waterproof and colorfast. In fact, several countries have already ordered samples. I figure everything based on the U.S. dollar, which is the currency of the world market. This claim cannot be made for the Shanghai dollar. We can produce everything very cheaply because the Chinese work for extremely low wages. They have a completely different standard of living and are content with small earnings that we could never do with even here. Women's silk underwear is also a good export item. Silk is inexpensive, and the most beautiful handwork . . . can be had for very little money. Aside from this, the Chinese have more patience than we Europeans. Asian calm is known throughout the world!

From the address book of the branches of the various underwear firms, I located the ones I wanted to visit. Those that were willing to do business with me, based on dollar value in addition to 10 percent for me, with these I decided to work. I delivered samples for sending abroad and am making some money without taking risks. Of course, I also visited a number of commercial representatives in order to discuss with them import fees. I also wanted to ascertain if . . . doing business with me would be profitable for the various countries. The export fees were a matter for the customs house here. I am very happy that I could discuss all these business arrangements in English. And I will not deny that I am enjoying this activity immensely, even if it involves great responsibility and is exhausting. Particularly nice and accommodating are the South African minister of commerce and the various persons responsible for American commerce. Until we begin to have a real income from these business enterprises, I have taken on the representation of an American insurance company as well as a hosiery business. I found the Chinese firms in the branch address book and figured 10 percent above the wholesale price. I am still cheaper than the stores because I have no overhead. I earn a little this way every day since everyone needs to wear hose. I also offer hose to the companies with which I concluded a transportation and insurance agreement because it sometimes takes weeks before the insurance fees are paid. One has to know how to manipulate the system! The expenses due to my husband's illness were enormous, and my greatest worry was how we would manage. The first thought upon rising and the last before falling asleep is: earn dollars. At times I don't recognize myself. After all, I was never that realistic. But now that I have lost my beautiful home and everything else, I am determined to create a real existence again, to get rid of the immigrant status, and to participate as quickly as possible in international business.

The children feel very well here. They attend a school where instruction is in English. Both were already advanced a grade. Aside from school, the second-wealthiest man in Shanghai, Mr. Kadoorie, a Sephardic Jew, has established a club that is in every way like a British youth club. Children attend the club three times a week for the entire afternoon. They are able to participate either in English conversation conducted by an English-woman, French lessons conducted by a Mademoiselle, or music lessons. Boys learn radio repair, play football, learn accounting, English stenography, jiu-jitsu, boxing, camp cooking, etc. Girls learn subjects that every well-brought-up person ought to know. The rooms are furnished in feudal style; children can go to the theater, to concerts, on hikes, hear English lectures; and all this is financially supported by Mr. Kadoorie, who loves children. He wants to see in the immigrant children's eyes once more the happiness and contentment that partially disappeared due to the emigration and the resulting inferiority complex. After they complete school, they should be able to speak perfect English. He has also committed himself to finding employment for all teenagers once they complete their studies. Parents pay a tiny sum of money for these generous offerings. You can see that much is done here especially for young people.

Now, in January, we have the most pleasant weather of the entire year, similar to Europe's beautiful month of May. I am sitting on our [enclosed] balcony, windows open, beautiful sunshine, thinking of you and the wonderful hours we spent together. Most likely we will never again have such a carefree feeling of permanence.

We continue to live in Hongkou, the Japanese section, where most of the immigrants live. It surely would be more interesting and pleasant to live in the International Settlement or the French Concession, but rents are too high there. For the time being we cannot afford this. Moreover, I am not home all day; my business is in the International Settlement and the French Concession, and in addition the children's school is close by and the air is also better here than in the city. Previously, before the Sino-Japanese War, the Americans and British who could afford it had villas in Hongkou. Now, of course, everything is under Japanese control and partially destroyed due to the hostilities. The immigrants were, therefore, often able to buy real estate cheaply and renovate buildings.

Whoever earns well can in fact forget that this is Asia and can live in European style. The most beautiful flats are available in Shanghai, villas, parks, theaters, movie houses, concerts, artists, American-style department stores with roof gardens. Shanghai is an international port city in the true sense of the word. Each time, I am enraptured anew by the highly interesting life around me. One simply must understand how to walk through this interesting city with open eyes, behold the lively goings-on and the international activity. There are the marvelous French fashion stores, skyscrapers like in America, colorful and interesting like nowhere else in the world. Asia and Europe meet everywhere. How I would like to show you everything. Sometimes I feel as if I actually live in a fairy tale. Recently we came across a bazaar in a typical Chinese neighborhood where we saw wonderful Chinese vases, jewelry, candelabras, small boxes, and colorful antiques. There were the various lit-up cabins in which the owners proudly praised their wares. Typically Oriental, and only two corners from there is the hum of the metropolis with its sophisticated everyday life. Bars are everywhere, places of entertainment, and in every street many beauty salons. International life is all around: Americans, British, Russians, Frenchmen, Indians, Germans, Chinese, and Japanese, the latter in their delightfully colorful clothes that too are reminiscent of a fairy tale.

You will laugh when I tell you that I only frequent Chinese beauty salons. They are the best as well as the preferred choice. First of all, the Chinese work for half the money European hairdressers demand, and, second, they are more skillful. No one can work as skillfully or cleanly as a Chinese, not to mention that included in the price are tea and cigarettes. They do not use combs, only ivory sticks, and manage to create with these the most sophisticated hair styles. . . . If only the climate were not so damp and the danger of infections not so great; if only the Chinese would not spit so much in buses, in the street, or in shops, Shanghai would be an ideal place. But, as you know, nothing in life is perfect, also not in Asia. Yet, despite all this, we are feeling extremely well here!!!!

New Year's Eve we spent delightfully with the other tenants in . . . the family room. We organized a picnic, had radio music for dancing, and an engineer from Stuttgart who lives here composed a theater piece about all of us. Peter, Marion, and our landlord's daughter presented it in a charming recitation. They wore costumes with makeup like real actors and actresses. It was certainly a successful evening. At exactly twelve o'clock the three children appeared as chimney sweeps, the electricity was turned off, and a poster by Peter with colorful lights appeared on the wall. It read, "A Happy New Year 1940."

For Christmas, there were wonderful exhibits in the various department stores, and I went with the children to the city to see them. We found them absolutely marvelous. To us, they seemed like a fairy tale, we felt as if enchanted. The wooden figures were full size, they were painted, and they moved; the forest and everything else were also full size, like in a dream.

Have I told enough, or is there still something you would like to know??? I forgot to mention how real estate rentals are transacted. Generally, the owner of a house is an American or Englishman who lives in the International Settlement or the French Concession. He rents the empty house for a relatively low price to someone for further rental. He does not concern himself further with the property and receives the rent each month. The person who rents the house from the original owner furnishes the rooms and rents each room separately [thus converting the house into a rooming house—ed.]. During the first years of the immigrants' arrival, earnings from rentals could be considerable. But today it is already harder to rent all the rooms in a house because many people lack the necessary funds. Many immigrants were forced to return to the "Heime" [home] because of the difficulty of finding work. Support from relatives abroad did not materialize and the immigration, for all practical purposes, came to a stop. That is the way a "house owner" looks in reality.

We went recently to the cinema and saw a wonderful film, *The Great Waltz*. It deals with the life of Johann Strauss, the king of waltz, and the children who went with us were also altogether enchanted.

In the morning, we often read in bed good books that we have borrowed from the library. Sometimes we go out, of course, or sit together with the other tenants in the common family room. They are lovely people and we get along nicely with them, as if we were one large family.

Only a few of the refugee physicians have succeeded here; there are too many in Shanghai. Those who have been in the city five, six, or seven years have steady patients, even Englishmen. But those who came at the same time as us depend on immigrant patients who cannot afford to pay much and sometimes not at all.

Your erstwhile home, dear Mrs. Alsberg, is certainly an unusually interesting and unique country that can be conquered but slowly. Will we Europeans ever be able to understand it???

Enough for today. To all of you many regards from us in old friendship from,

Annie Witting

Readers of this letter can gain an excellent picture of how a displaced family managed despite illness, strange and unaccustomed surroundings, and inexperience. To be sure, the Wittings had some financial support from Annie's brother, Heinz Wilhelm, who by then was in South Africa. Nonetheless, one cannot but admire the energetic spirit of this woman who tackled a number of business enterprises to provide a living. Aside from work, there were also lighter moments. She tells us about enjoying Christmas decorations, the New Year celebration, the occasional movie, and, above all, the fact that her children were usefully occupied in school and in the Kadoorie club. Today we might find her comments about Chinese workers disagreeable. But we should remember that, then as now, Chinese labor was cheap and the Chinese worker was exploited. She is stating a fact of life and she is concerned with how to make a living for her family.

The reader also has occasional glimpses of contacts with the Chinese population. Apparently, Witting, as well as others, ventured into the Chinese areas of Shanghai, and often there is a sense of wonder, indeed, even adventure of encountering the strange and wonderful city. Although few social contacts were ever established, the horror of culture shock is not evident in this or her other letters. They do not deal, as do a number of memoirs written at a later time, with Shanghai's unsanitary conditions, the ubiquitous vermin, or the foul smells.[68]

Unfortunately, the outbreak of the Pacific War in December 1941 ended all correspondence among Shanghai, Europe, and America. Given Witting's ability to observe and describe, a contemporary record of how the Wittings managed during the war would have been invaluable. But all we have is a postscript to this letter, added apparently after the Wittings left Shanghai in 1947. There is no date, and since this is not really part of the letter, I shall only summarize her comments and not translate.

Until the outbreak of the Pacific War, both Witting and her husband managed quite well financially. He worked as a cashier and bookkeeper at an American export company, and she continued her work as an agent for a number of business enterprises. She remarks perceptively that, instead of teaching the Chinese how to conduct business, Europeans learned business routine from the Chinese. The war years were, however, exceedingly difficult for them with commercial life and export business at a near standstill. Still, the children continued to prosper. Peter, she tells us, wants to become a mechanical engineer, and Marion studied at a commercial school, following which she worked as a secretary.

* LOTTE MARGOT (?) *

It was impossible to ascertain who the author of this interesting short piece is, or when she came to Shanghai. Wilfried Seywald mentions a Lotte Margot with the surname of Sussmann.[69] Presumably she was a typist and contributor to the *8-Uhr Abendblatt*. Since the article is signed "Lotte Margot," I assume that Sussmann is the author.

∿

THE CHINESE WOMAN DANCES (1940)[70]

Bubbling Well Road. The coolie jerks to a halt and stops in front of The Majestic across from the racecourse. The Majestic is the largest dance hall in Shanghai. The narrow staircase does not lead one to suspect that above is a gigantic oval hall, around which girls are perched on minuscule folding chairs, almost too small for sitting. There are so many Chinese girls in their slit gowns that it is impossible to count them all. Tables for guests surround the dance floor. The band begins to roar and the young Chinese jump up. Each fetches a girl.

They dance joyfully, not as in Europe and not as in America. Most of the young men are students, and the girls look like children. None of the "taxi girls" is more than twenty years old. Female students are also here, and they too fetch a [taxi girl] partner like the men to enjoy the dance. Now it starts in earnest, frenzied rocking and swinging, while the long gowns fly away from the legs of the young beaming Chinese girls. But a European must see and understand this correctly because this is not a "market of love." The hall is at all times an utterly decent and proper place. The dancers consider the movement of feet and the swaying in time an art. They move away from one another, find each other again in artistic configurations. Throughout, their faces remain unapproachable, as if these were the first moments of an English college tea that included dancing. Chinese girls take enormous pleasure in dance, but at the same time exhibit the restraint that all previous dynasties declared to be a female duty.

Together with the music the lights also change; purple and shimmering green alternate with the red and yellow of the gowns worn by the girls. A rhythm pervades the dance hall, a rhythm that was invented in America, but one that these children have adopted with assurance and certainty. The rhythm became domesticated and has become Chinese like the Indian Buddha a millennium earlier. A vast divide separates Chinese music from this controlled and trumpeted jazz. Yet it seems to have become part of these young peoples' being, somehow ennobled as the "Broadway people" have not managed to do. . . .

Four o'clock in the morning. From the window of my room I see in the street a Chinese girl, perhaps ten, at most twelve years of age. She wears long black pants and a short blue shirt. She runs to everyone she sees trying to sell the morning newspaper. A beggar with wildly glazed eyes accosts a foreigner, "Mister, I am starving!" Only a moment ago, the foreigner had thrown forty, fifty, one hundred dollars on a brightly polished bar, but the beggar does not even get five cents.

One has become used to them, one hardly sees [the beggars] anymore. I too will pass them by. But . . . after a few steps, I will see the pale, hungry face of the Chinese man. My God, I am no different from that foreigner. Time to go to bed.

The author provides in this brief essay a rare glimpse of the "other Shanghai." These are the affluent, the well-to-do Chinese students, she assumes, who have taken to American jazz and frequent dance halls. This is the Shanghai that Langston Hughes (1902–1967) visited in 1933 and about which he remarked that the Chinese "seemed to have a weakness for American Negro performers" and American jazz.[71] According to Lotte Margot, no impropriety of any sort can be perceived in The Majestic, where dancing to jazz music is enjoyed as much by the women as by the men. The women may be dance hall hostesses, hired for the entertainment of customers, but they are not prostitutes, nor do they solicit.

Yet the author is either too innocent or too intent on conveying a positive image of the dance hall in Shanghai life. Dance halls became popular in the 1920s, and there were high-class establishments as well as those frequented by the lower classes, even those frequented by foreigners. There is no question that social dancing, a Western custom introduced in the nineteenth century, was enthusiastically embraced by Shanghai's urbanites. However, whether the taxi dancers enjoyed dancing as much as the author would want the reader to believe is questionable. Taxi dancing was an opportunity to earn an income at a time when precious few such opportunities (except for menial factory work) were open to women. Although this income was most likely contributed to the family, a woman's earning power also gave her a measure of independence. The dance hall, cinema, and other such public spaces transformed Shanghai into the unique city of contrasts, of rich and poor, that this piece manages to capture.[72]

Finally, articles such as this one, or the ones by Willy Tonn, afford the reader a tiny glimpse of the variety of materials that were published in the German exile press. Apparently, however, there were very few refugee women journalists in Shanghai and no assumptions can be made about aspects of Shanghai life, different from those observed by men, that may have caught women's attention.

* E. SIMKHONI *

(SIMKHA ELBERG, 1915?–1995)[73]

Rabbi Simkha Elberg was a prestigious scholar of rabbinic law, a subject on which he published prolifically in addition to other Talmudic
topics. He probably did not come to Shanghai as a member of the Mir
Yeshiva,[74] and may have come independently as did some others. Aside
from the poetry published in *Undzer lebn* (Our life), he also contributed regularly to *Dos vort* (The word, fig. 6, above), signing his name
sometimes as Simkhoni-Elberg. The paper, in Yiddish and English, described itself as "A Jewish Weekly for the Religious Revival in the Far
East." In Shanghai, he met and married Miriam Slutzker, who hailed
from Harbin and was the daughter of the well-known Lithuanian rabbi
Yehuda Zelig Slutzker. Both Elberg and his wife came to New York in
1947, where he embarked on a successful career as rabbi and author.
After he passed away, his widow carried on energetically until her death.
Husband and wife are buried in Jerusalem.

❧

THREE COUNTRIES SPAT ME OUT (1941)[75]

Three countries spat me out,
as a dead body is spat out
by stormy seas.

My home, Poland,
locked in a ghetto, entombed,
I don't know who prays "Rakhamim" in his need,
who whispers "Sh'ma Yisrael" quietly,
praying for death.

My stepmother Lithuania lauded Mickiewicz,
when a red sun rose on the Nieman River,

not one tear did the river swallow
where the red banner fluttered.

One white day of snow,
I escaped in fright,
and because my day did not have a red spot
Lithuania spat me out,
as one who is tubercular spits
his last bit of blood.

In Japan I made ink from the sea,
from heaven a white sheet of paper,
even the wind did groan
when I wrote: send me a visa!

On a humid day,
when the Japanese tie up their nose
and step with wooden feet,
Japan spat me out
into Shanghai.

There is not an ounce of self-pity here, but rather anger and worry about those left behind, as if already consigned to death. Jewish custom demands that the poet recite the prayers associated with dying and the dead, but in his next breath he cannot help but refer sarcastically to the Lithuanians who praise their national poet, Adam Mickiewicz, yet shed no tears when the red flag of the newly arrived Russian army is raised. The poet lets us know that he escaped in the nick of time, had to flee, not wanting, or not being able, to live under Russian domination, landing this time in Japan. There he could not remain either, and the hoped-for travel documents to elsewhere were not forthcoming.

The strong emotions expressed in the poem are carefully arranged throughout the six verses. The first introduces the forceful ejection of the poet and the second verse repeatedly refers to death and the dying of those left behind. The third and fourth verses stress colors: the red flag, red blood, white snow. The fifth verse continues the color motif, black ocean, white paper, but also introduces a sense of timelessness and waiting for the visa that never seems to come. The last verse, the poet's last impression of his temporary home, is an image of Japanese with surgical masks to guard against infection and wearing the characteristic wooden clogs.[76]

✳ KURT LEWIN ✳

(PSEUD. KLEWING, 1908–1950?)[77]
An anti-fascist who fled from Berlin to Shanghai in 1939, Lewin worked
on various German newspapers published in his new home, most of
them short-lived, except for the *Shanghai Jewish Chronicle*. He is generally identified as a journalist, writer, and actor. Unlike the Yiddish
poets, Lewin tended to write satirical poetry, the last poems appear-
ing in 1946 as "Der Wochensalat" (The weekly salad). He returned to
Germany in 1947, living first in East Germany and then moving to the
West. In Germany, he authored radio plays. In 1943 he published a book
of essays, *Shanghai und wir,* which seems to be unavailable in any of the
known libraries.

⌇

MORE LIGHT (1941)[78]

The house of woe, 'tis Goethe's final moment,
Deeply affected mourners hearken
To words of sagely comment.
His exhortation barely heard:
"More light!"

In our world, in countries everywhere,
Wherever still are free men,
A shout echoes from every side:
"More light!"

Freedom of thought is every street's demand,
We may be loved or may be hated.
From our call only the worthless hide:
"More light!"

We strive for neither stars nor bright sun's gloss,
Thousands of "lanterns" gleam amid the city's dross.
A scoundrel he who by his promise won't abide
"More light!"

We work for you with pleasure well fulfilled,
And you "lantern" after "lantern" help us build
Until their bright lights penetrate all hearts.
Help us awaken sleepers from their rest,
To find the "Lantern" shining bright,
Heed our call:
"More light!"

When darkness began to envelop Asia, the thirty-two-year-old Kurt Lewin, on the occasion of the newly established weekly, *Die Laterne* (The lantern, fig. 9, above) called for more light. Although Lewin wrote poems for all subsequent issues (I have only seen issues from June 14 to July 7, 1941), "More Light" can be considered representative. *Die Laterne*, subtitled "Weekly for Free Intellectual Creativity," was a most interesting paper for the variety of high-quality materials published in its pages and for the opportunity it provided for readers to express their views on everyday occurrences. The poem translated here is especially moving because of its optimistic—perhaps better, defiant—message. As World War II swept across the planet, Lewin pleaded for spiritual and intellectual illumination. An astute observer of the current scene (as in another poem written five years later and translated below), he could not have failed to notice the gathering war clouds around Shanghai. Five months or so before the start of the Pacific War, fewer ships had begun to dock at Shanghai wharves; not a good sign now that Italy had joined the war on Hitler's side and the German armies had begun to invade Soviet Russia.

Yet despite these dire developments, the new weekly paper was born and Lewin began "More Light" by reminding his readers of the great man of German letters whose tradition they are obliged to carry forward. At least two meanings must, therefore, be attributed to this poem. On the one hand, the enlightened spirit of the past represented by the German poet must continue to live. On the other, there is the hope that this weekly paper, *Die Laterne*, will ignite other lanterns to shine brightly in the gathering darkness. Professor Joshua Fogel's comment on this poem is significant. He writes: "I sensed here the subliminal image of Diogenes traveling about with a lantern looking for an honest man."[79]

Exile was, for German intellectuals like Lewin, a complex problem. They were proud German Jews, usually not religiously observant, who had completely internalized German culture. The German poets, Goethe and Schiller, or the composers, Mozart and Beethoven, were better known to them than the greats of Jewish tradition. Germany had rejected its Jewish populace, caused them to flee for their lives into exile, not so much for what they believed as for who they were by virtue of birth. The Jews did not, however, reject German literature and music. Bending Goethe to his own purposes, Lewin transforms the German poet into a harbinger of reason and enlightenment at a time of chaos.

* YEHOSHUA RAPOPORT *

(1895–1971)

Yehoshua Rapoport was a highly respected and well-known literary critic, essayist, and translator from Russian, German, English, French, and Hebrew into Yiddish. He was born in Białystok and lived in Berlin as well as Warsaw. In 1941 he came to Shanghai via Lithuania and Kobe with one of the Polish groups. In 1946, after the end of war, he settled in Melbourne, Australia.

His literary activity began in the 1930s, when he published a number of books in addition to publishing widely in the Yiddish press. In Shanghai he was a frequent contributor to the Yiddish page of *Nasha Zhizn* (Our life), and in 1941, despite tremendous difficulties, he published in English *Der mahut fun dikhtung un ir sotsiale funktsye* (The very essence of poetry and its social function). The manuscript for this book, he tells us in the introduction, was left behind in Warsaw. The reconstructed manuscript that he had worked on in Vilna was once more left behind when he fled to Kobe. The second reconstruction in Shanghai was done without the benefit of books, for they were not available.[80]

In Melbourne he was finally able to pursue a vigorous publishing career. Many people may have disagreed with the high moral standards Rapoport demanded of himself and others. But, in the words of Meylekh Ravitch, "Rapoport was widely read because one learned from him."[81]

❧

AND SO IT BEGINS . . . (JEWISH CULTURAL
WORK IN SHANGHAI) (1941)[82]

. . . People run from destruction and pogroms and, on the way, plant a settlement here, a little spiritual [content] there, with which to animate an atrophied limb. But the present human characteristic has almost become second nature with Jews: who else has run from destruction as much as we Jews? And who has planted our spiritual goods and new settlements in all corners of the world as often as we have?

. . . .

A quarter century ago the dual storm of war and revolution brought a few Jews to East Asia. Jewish life began to breathe weakly and anemically in Harbin, Tianjin, and Shanghai. There were Jewish libraries, clubs, lectures, and performances. There was even a Yiddish newspaper in Harbin.

The Jewish pulse, however, grew ever weaker. No transfusions of new blood were available; a part of the Jewish blood that had been brought along dried up due to emigration; the rest atrophied due to anemia. The red corpuscles of Jewish blood lost their resistance, although one might have thought that once there had been an attempt at Jewish life to strike roots in East Asia. However, as it turned out, it was still too early to say kaddish [the prayer for the dead—ed.]. . . . Storm no. 2 again drove a small Jewish community to East Asia. And perhaps we are witnessing the timid beginnings of a miracle: Jewish life in East Asia begins again, it shows signs of Jewish strength and resistance.

It is told that when archeologists opened one of the pyramids, a few wheat kernels were found that had dried out in the thousands of years they were buried. But a little earth and sunshine were enough for the dry kernels to sprout. Their inner vitality sufficed to preserve them for centuries. The Jewish seed contains no less vitality. No matter how dried out it is on the outside, within lies dormant Jewish vitality that is prepared to . . . come to life.

We came to Shanghai as if to a dead kingdom, as if an evil power had transformed into stone everything that was truly Jewish. Still, our despairing screams were enough to remove from this stone the evil . . . curse. There, where it was assumed all was waste, stone, and cold, something began to thaw. . . . Like in the fairy tale where the . . . [prince] only has to prove himself for the princess to awaken.

. . . .

Thus the miracle simply begins.

Thus it begins.

A Jewish journalist comes to Shanghai and naturally wants to continue his journalistic career. He wanders about town and writes eleven pages in Russian in order to have one small page in Yiddish. The page looks poor, almost ridiculous, as if begging to be destroyed harking back to destruction. One would like to cry out in a bitter moment: better nothing! It is understandable, one can empathize, but it is not right. Injustice would be done.

That small page looks superfluous, it is not read much, but for the few in number it is singularly important among the twelve pages. Readers turn the pages over time and again . . . and those who yell that a Yiddish page is not needed become accustomed to its existence. The page becomes a fact for which room must be made, a little room, a life.

How was this possible in Shanghai?

God, they say, heals before the scourge.

Two weeks before the outbreak of war the Jews here received some Yiddish written matter from Warsaw . . . that did not rest a minute. A four-page Yiddish newspaper was soon typeset . . . as well as a pamphlet of sixty-four pages and a collection of thirty-two pages.

How was this possible in Shanghai?

Again, the same: God heals before the scourge. How does a tree or a flower grow in a mountain of stone? The wind brings a little soil, the soil collects, and together with the soil the seeds of various plants accumulate.

The storm that brought to Shanghai a fragmented Jewish host also brought Jewish writers, cultural activists, and a Yiddish typesetter. . . . Together with the written word one can now also hear Yiddish words spoken in Shanghai. In the beginning there was the Shanghai ditty:

A new sensation in Shanghai
listen, listen, be astonished.
It seems that Jews have arrived
and they even speak Yiddish!

In the beginning Shanghai Jews could not suffer this. . . . They were forever afraid that nobody would come to hear a lecture in Yiddish because no one understands the language. Another claim was that to give a Yiddish lecture in Shanghai is as difficult as "splitting the Red Sea" [a reference to Moses, who divided the Red Sea so that the Israelites could flee Egypt—ed.].

But the effort was not in vain. After the first lecture came a second and third, and now there is already a forum of three hundred with the attendance growing. The Yiddish word is now no longer only spoken, people sing and recite in Yiddish. We even grabbed a radio station and we have Yiddish broadcasts three times a week. To Shanghai came a lively Yiddish element, and Jewish life breathes more strongly and is growing. Different sounds are heard, the Jewish Club is happy because its first cultural offering in its new location was in Yiddish and the club's culture committee hopes that its activities will increasingly include Yiddish offerings. . . . Moreover, people who insisted they don't know Yiddish suddenly discovered extraordinary linguistic abilities and in a short time learned to speak Yiddish! And those who usually rejected Yiddish, because in Shanghai Yiddish is not needed, is not known, are now intent on publishing a Yiddish newspaper or a Yiddish book.

. . . .

. . . Nobody does anything for someone else. Whatever one does is for oneself. Our cultural work that we want to do here is also in accordance with our need. We are not doing you [Shanghai people] a favor because what for you is merely refreshing is for us like the air we breathe. A work environment, collective existence, is the highest and probably the only way to live humanly like a human being. But don't do us a favor either because you need Yiddish culture as much as we, maybe even more than we. We feel uncomfortable in your cultural environment, but we feel within ourselves the cultural ties to our tortured home. . . . We still feel sharply our new uprooted condition and we are no longer nourished by roots [of our home]. However, we have brought along sufficient nourishment . . . for our severed and homeless life. You may no longer feel the pain of being uprooted. But I cannot believe you are unfeeling, that you have no roots, and that the root of your tree is dry. I cannot believe it—I see the worry in your eyes. When you look at your children, or when you talk about them, I see that you still value stray Yiddish books. Even if such books are not living nourishment that you need every day and are more like relics that one values but no longer uses.

You now have a chance to abandon, at least, a small portion of your orphaned state. You have the chance to expose your children to an electric shock through contact . . . with a still living organism. We don't want favors from you, nor do we want to do you favors. We only long for mutual work with you because it is a mutual necessity. That is our aim and that is the meaning of our modest work.

Thus it always begins.

And this is the way it began.

Rapoport wrote this essay shortly after his arrival in Shanghai. It is at first glance an optimistic statement about Jewish life, despite the indifferent welcome he and his fellow refugees received. Jewish and Yiddish culture is, in his view, an organism nourished by blood and air. When both are present, it will develop and grow. When both are lacking, Jewish culture will die and disappear. Yet, he also compared Jewish culture to a dry kernel that can be revived, that is miraculously capable of striking new roots when planted in congenial soil. In this essay, Rapoport sees his own function and that of others like him in Shanghai as contributing to a revival and of bringing new life.

This was not presumption on his part. Rapoport considered himself an heir to a long tradition of Yiddish culture, a genuine culture of Jewry. Shanghai Jews were already far removed from that tradition, according to him. Interestingly, he did not take into account the Sephardic Jewish tradition, which was, after all, also a part of Shanghai life. However, he cannot be faulted for this, for in Poland and Eastern Europe the Sephardic tradition had, for all practical purposes, blended into Yiddish culture.

Unlike Shanghai Jewry, to whom Yiddish culture was already a relic of the past, Rapoport suggests that, through common effort and cooperation between previous inhabitants and newcomers, Jewish culture can be made to flourish, if not for this generation then for the future. It can live, he optimistically assured his readers, as long as a small particle of vitality is present. He was not only the harbinger of new life, but actually carried with him, or more accurately brought along, a kernel of this new life.

✳ *YOSL MLOTEK* ✳

(1918–2000)[83]

Yosl (Joseph) Mlotek was born in the small Polish town of Proszomice, and moved with his parents to Warsaw at the age of seven. The Mlotek family was a large one, with six boys and two girls. Mlotek had a secular education; at a young age he joined the Jewish socialist movement, and began writing and publishing poetry at the age of twelve. According to his own account, he published his poetry regularly in the Bundist paper *Folkstsaytung* (People's newspaper).[84] In September 1939, he fled first to Vilna, Lithuania, making his way with the group of Polish-Jewish writers who went first to Japan and then to Shanghai. Mlotek was twenty-three years old when they arrived in Shanghai on August 30, 1941, on the *Tatuta Maru*.[85]

Two of the poems translated here, "The Lament of My Mother" and "A Letter," speak of the loneliness of the young man who, having left home when he was twenty-one years old, had lived among strangers ever since. The third poem, "Shanghai," is different. Here the poet does not describe his own condition or frame of mind. Rather, like Meylekh Ravitch before him, he reaches out to the Chinese people—the Shanghai of painful and barely human contrasts in which they exist—and tells his readers that their lot is far worse than that of the refugees.

In 1947, Mlotek left Shanghai, going first to Canada, then to New York in 1949. There he taught high school and continued to write for Yiddish publications, becoming an important figure in Yiddish education and folklore. One of the Jewish papers described him as a "towering figure of his generation."[86]

〜

THE LAMENT OF MY MOTHER (1941)[87]

Through oceans and countries,
Through closures and walls,
I see my mother's
Cracked hands.

I hear my mother's
Sobs and laments
—Where are my children
Lost and alone?

I hear her sobs,
Am aware of her grief
And each painful tear
Like a stone on my path.

My foolish heart
Races back toward home.
The heart knows no borders
Or artificial fences.

The heart knows no structures
Protected by guards.
Break down the gate,
I'm at her door.

I meet my mother
Already old with grey hair.
She hugs me, a caress,
And says:

"Flown away, flown afar like birds in autumn,
Tell, my children, my life, to that land.
Only yesterday have I rocked your cradle
Singing songs for you about golden happiness.

Today you flew away like leaves in the wind,
Already you're homesick, is it the truth my child?
Good, at least you've returned
To my dreams, my longing, my golden happiness."

Together I was
With mother.
No longer solitary
No longer alone.

I feel every tear that drops
On me like a blow.
Only at mother's side is it good—
Good, so . . . good. . . .

Yosl Mlotek wrote "The Lament of My Mother" either before he arrived
in Shanghai or shortly after he reached China in summer or early fall
1941. The loneliness of the young man is palpable in the poem. Unlike
the poems below, which are full of color and movement, here are no colors, save for his mother's grey hair. The poet seems imprisoned behind
walls, structures (the Yiddish actually reads "outer walls"), gates protected by guards. All he can do is send his heart racing homeward, for
only the heart need pay no attention to obstacles. But it is more than
homesickness, longing for family and familiar places, that can be heard
in the poem. There is also concern for loved ones with whom all contact was lost by 1941. To be sure, news from Poland trickled through to
Shanghai; there was the English-language press and the Russian news
service at the Soviet embassy. But this was not personal news. The Polish
refugees, when they met one another, must have agonized over the fate
of their loved ones.

* E. SIMKHONI *

MY GOD, MY GOD, WHY HAST THOU FORSAKEN ME" (1942)[88]

Why God, have you abandoned me
And extinguished your light.
Rain outside
And all rooms are locked with no key.
If not you, who can answer me outright?
When night fell
You and all others mocked me.

In back of the book the mite eats till full.
The worm sleeps quietly in its terrestrial bed.
To me you gave as a friend the street
Where it is dark, full of sleet.

In your holy books it is written:
"Heaven for God, earth for men."
So why must I remain forsaken.

Japan's attack on Pearl Harbor and the start of the Pacific War must have been a crushing blow to the refugees, who were now totally cut off from Europe. In this short poem, written no doubt as soon as war began on December 8, 1941, and with the Japanese occupying all of Shanghai, Simkhoni speaks for all the refugees. Only worms can still exist in peace; for other creatures darkness has fallen and all doors have been closed. God has abandoned the unfortunates, indeed, makes fun of their misery. Simkhoni took the poem's title from Psalm 22:1, which begins "Eli, Eli lamah azavtani."

Simkhoni was a religious man and he must have been well acquainted with this long psalm. Two other images from the psalm appear in his poem, though the context is entirely different in the first case. One is the worm in verse 7: "I am a worm and no man." The other is being scorned or mocked in verse 8: "I am scorned by all who see me." The implication in the psalm is that he is mocked as one who believed.

The theme of abandonment at the time of great calamity is common to both the psalm and Simkhoni's poem. However, where the last nine verses of the psalm hold out hope and praise the Lord, Simkhoni ends his poem on a note of despair. He and his people remain forsaken, as well he might have felt at the outbreak of war between the U.S. and Japan.

✳ *MORDECHAI ROTENBERG* ✳

(b. 1920)[89]
The poet Mordechai Rotenberg was born into a rabbinic family in Poland, and was a student in the Mir Yeshiva. He must have left Poland
with the Mir group in 1939, going first to Kobe, and arrived in Shanghai
with them later. Rotenberg left for New York in 1946 and taught at Yeshiva University. His poems have appeared in New York Yiddish journals. Mordechai Rotenberg lives today in Brooklyn.

SUN IN A NET (1942)[90]

Sun's rays
in motherly ways
fall
on soft
flat plains
and—smile.

Melodious songs,
nets spread to catch throngs
of fish,
but out of bounds they run.

The chase is on
of nets after fish. . . .
Meanwhile rays from the sun
run
from the plain
to fill the net.

14. Qi Baishi, "Fishes." From Lubor Hajek et al., *Contemporary Chinese Painting* (London: Spring Books, 1961), p. 67.

15. Li Xiongcai, "On the Lu Mountains." From Lubor Hajek et al., *Contemporary Chinese Painting* (London: Spring Books, 1961), p. 119.

Angrily fishermen
mutter:
Rays instead fish?
A devilish joke.

And I—
would give many a day
for a sun's ray. . . .

The impetus for the poem may have been paintings of fish, with or without fishermen, a favorite motif of traditional and often even modern Chinese painting (figs. 14 and 15). Or perhaps the poet remembered fish and fishermen from his days in Kobe. It would also seem that some religious school students were not as otherworldly as we tend to believe, for the twenty-two-year-old student most likely continued to live with the Mir yeshiva students and rabbis. We can assume this because *Di yidishe shtime* (The Jewish voice) was a paper of the religious Orthodox (Aguda) movement and a means for expressing rabbinic views. Rotenberg does not speak in this poem of longing for home, or the family he has left behind. But the poem does express a longing for hope, perhaps foremost on the minds of refugees at the time because, by the summer of 1942, the war was not going well for the allies and the Shanghai refugees were completely cut off from Europe.

✳ *YOSL MLOTEK* ✳

SHANGHAI (1942)[91]

Shanghai—
The city beckons
With a thousand passionate eyes.
Neon lights dazzle
A marvelous rainbow.

Changing colors, moving
Glittering mercury.
Up and down, down and up—
An electric thunderstorm.

—Buy, buy these cigars
The brand "Two Times F"!
—Women don't be fooled
Silks, socks, the brand "Blef."

On houses
On roofs
On chimneys
And still higher—
Buy! Buy!

Signal lights,
Messages
Call and pull, allure
Remind and caress
Buy! Buy!
And at the side
Runs
A man in harness—a horse,

Feet barely touch the ground.
Behind him—ten, hundreds more
Run, hurry, noisily.
They must run faster, faster—
Otherwise how to be sure
Though at night he runs
Even twenty times in a circle
Whether there'll be
A small bowl of rice.

— — — — — —

"Your eyes, your glances
 have caught me"—
He fell into the street, there he lays
Drunken sounds—

"International Bar"
 —Enter
 —Whisky, beer?
 —Well I prefer liquor. . . .

 —How nicely you dance this waltz . . .
  One, two, three
  One, two, three
 —I kiss your swan-like neck
  One, two, three
  One, two, three
 Please not so rigid,
 Not nice like this . . . the guests
 —But you have strange
 eyes . . .
 Not here. My room—higher . . .
 upstairs . . .
  One, two, three
  One, two, three
 "International Bar" . . . —

And outside
"Dear Sir, Sir,
I have not eaten so long . . .
Shadows at the wall
Pale hands are thrust:
Mister, food . . . food. . . . "

Above—jazz music
And drunken laughter.
Below a tight cluster
China's daughters
Stand at the wall
Together with their mothers.
And above mocking them
A large lit advertisement:
Buy! Buy!

Shanghai
Nanking Road
The city screams
From a thousand throats
And from a thousand eyes.
Ever louder, shriller
Shouts resound
Scream China! Shanghai, scream!

Mlotek's poem pictures Nanking Road, the heart of the International Settlement, with its advertisements, its bars and glitter, its rickshaw coolies and its prostitutes. But Nanking Road was only for the wealthy Chinese and Westerners of Shanghai who frequented its elegant shops and restaurants. Soon the Westerners would be gone, their places taken by the Japanese, who occupied the International Settlement in December 1941. As in his previous poems, here again is the rich imagery, now of flashing advertisements, of blinding lights, of noise, but also of desperation. No matter how fast the coolie runs he seems always on the verge of starvation. Mlotek's final sentence echoes the sense of despair of Chinese poets and writers at the time, not only because of the cruelties of war, or China's impotence in the face of Japanese aggression. They despaired, too, of China's poverty and her backwardness. It is highly unlikely that Jewish and Chinese poets knew one another, were aware of each other, or read each other's works. Yet the stirrings of the heart, born of the quality of compassion for fellow human beings, was certainly common to them.[92]

Like Mlotek, Meylekh Ravitch in "A Rickshaw Coolie Dies on a Shanghai Dawn," translated above, expresses compassion for those more unfortunate than he. But Ravitch had not experienced forced exile and homelessness the way Mlotek had. Mlotek's path to Shanghai was quite different, less favorable or pleasant than was Ravitch's. However, both poets, I think, managed to listen to what the Chinese philosopher, Mencius (Meng Ko, 371–289 BCE?), called "the heart of mercy" (*buren renzhi xin, Mengzi* 2A:6). Jacob Fishman, whose "Miniatures" is translated below, should be added to Ravitch and Mlotek for expressing a similar sentiment. Fishman and Mlotek were acquainted in Shanghai, according to Yehoshua Rapoport's diary. One would have liked to eavesdrop on the conversations the two might have had about the city, its Chinese inhabitants, and its immigrant culture.

(?–?)

Except that he was an actor and entertainer, nothing is known about
Karl Heinz Wolff.

❧

THE DILIGENT MASON (1942)[93]

I have a house in Shanghai, 'tis like new,
In the recent shooting something went askew,
A few stones are missing,
New ones are needed,
I speak to a mason, will new stones fit?
Of course, says the man, that's it,
Tomorrow morning we start.
Eight o'clock comes and goes,
An hour later he's here,
I say, 'tis late, no, he does say,
The time's just right,
Long is the road and I live far away,
No tramway was to be had,
Walking on foot was not too bad.
He starts, he looks, thoughtfully, exact,
Unpacks what he thought was required.
Looks up at the house, a stone's obviously needed,
Picks up the stone and puts it away unheeded.
He finds the ladder to climb to the top,
He carries it eight feet, then the clock strikes ten.
Breakfast time now, he eats what he can
Then lights his pipe that doesn't stay lit,
Takes a brief nap when the clock strikes again.
He picks up the stone, the same as before,
But he must sneeze, his head's not quite right,

Puts the stone away for he's taken a fright.
He looks for a kerchief but finds none.
I say
It's okay
And give him mine.
Now he feels good, like a fish far from shore,
He takes a stone, the same as before
And goes to the ladder when the clock strikes twelve.
Well, the stone's put aside,
His wife comes with a bite,
After so much work it tastes really good.
She sits next to him, he sits next to her,
They eat cucumbers, potatoes, and drink liquor.
Now he must read the news and angrily shouts,
They're striking again, like us they should work.
He gives her a kiss, and closes his eyes,
Then the clock strikes two and he must rise.
He mixes cement that's yellow and soft,
He picks up the stone, the same as before,
But after the meal his stomach is sore.
He puts down the stone, takes the paper he's read
And goes to the W.C. instead.
He reappears when the clock strikes three,
Picks up the stone that's none other than prior
And goes to the ladder filled with new fire.
Twenty rungs has the ladder, but he is unwearied,
On the eighteenth he stops when four strikes the clock
Neither up nor down, he's out of luck.
His tariff will not let him advance the two rungs,
Eighteen down with the stone may imperil his life.
What to do when so close to accomplishment,
He hesitates between work and how to be diligent.
Diligence wins, all the same, he's now mad,
Lets the stone fall precisely on my head.
Why do you stand here?, he says, as I scold and grumble,
You don't need your head to do work that's humble.

∾

The comedy expressed in Wolff's poem, of a bewildered German émigré observing the seeming inefficiency of a Shanghai mason's work habits, is a welcome antidote to the pathos of the other writings gathered in this book. We share the poet's amusement at the situation, and the knowledge that the mason is actually not an uneducated clod: he reads the newspaper, eats nourishing food, observes union rules. In the end, nationality or ethnic difference is less important than the way Wolff's use of "diligence" (careful, methodical, and slow!) in the poem's title cuts two ways: the mason is not the archetypal "mysterious Oriental" but a rather shrewd worker whom one might encounter anywhere, perfectly capable of doing the work in less time, but preferring to stretch the job out. After all, he'll get paid his day's wage, every day, for as many days as the job lasts.

The poem was submitted to the Shanghai Municipal Police as part of an entertainment program planned for Jewish Refugee Camp at 961 Seward Road. The police, evidently, approved the program since, as stated in their report of March 19, 1942, "nothing of an objectionable notice has been observed."

∗ *HERMANN GOLDFARB* ∗

(?–?)
Sadly, nothing is known of Goldfarb except that he lived in Shanghai during this period.

WANDERING (1942)[94]

I
Wander Jew, wander, roam,
For you only a shabby tent.
Nowhere is a peaceful home,
Move on, wander in the world.

II
Condemned to ramble
Even in the hoary past.
Remember the Egyptian gamble,
You lost and fled in the Red Sea.

III
And later when the sword of Rome
Destroyed your state,
You set forth once more to roam,
From land to land.

IV
Never more will you find rest,
Ever onward you must move.
Always only as a guest,
No use trying to remain.

V

Wander Jews, roam afar,
These the words that greet you.
Under moon and under star,
Go on roaming, go away.

VI

How much farther need they range,
Over oceans and through states,
To endure what's odd and strange,
Why submit to hardship thus?

VII

Open your eyes at last,
New world that's civilized.
Release us from suffering vast,
Bring us the calm we need.

Hermann Goldfarb's poem, apparently also presented at a variety evening, stands in sharp contrast to the poem by Karl Heinz Wolff, "The Diligent Mason." If both poems were recited as entertainment, then one would have induced chuckles, the other would have reminded the audience of its suffering. The wandering Jew theme—often cited in Christian sources as punishment for the deed of crucifixion—had become internalized as the Jewish condition of homelessness. To the Shanghai refugees, this theme was preeminently meaningful. They had wandered to what seemed the farthest reaches of the earth, yet they knew that once the conflagration in Europe was over they would not remain in China. Once again they would have to pick up and go. The poet chides a so-called "civilized" world that tolerates homelessness and suffering, but gestures toward a "new world," presumably Australia or the U.S., where some of the Shanghai Jews moved after the war.

✴ JACOB H. FISHMAN ✴

(1891–1965)[95]

Jacob Fishman (fig. 16) was born in the Polish town of Szedlec, where he received a religious education, as did most boys his age. He began writing at an early age and published his first short story in 1910. Later he lived on and off in Warsaw, where he was a teacher of Hebrew and Yiddish. Fishman left Poland at the outbreak of World War II, fleeing first to Lithuania, then to Shanghai with the group of Polish-Jewish writers. Like the writings of Meylekh Ravitch and Yosl Mlotek, Fishman's prose sketches reveal a compassion for the downtrodden and oppressed Chinese people. Among the several collections of short stories by Fishman, *Farvoglte yidn* (Homeless Jews) was published in Shanghai.[96] It contains five tales about Shanghai life, one of which, "A Wedding," translated for this collection, appears below. Fishman left China in 1948 for Montreal, eventually settling in New York in 1950.

16. Jacob H. Fishman (19??). *Frier un shpeter, dertseylungen* (Earlier and later: stories) (Buenos Aires: Gezelshaft far yidish-weltlikhe shuln in Argentine, 1957).

MINIATURES (1942)[97]

At a café window sits a highly satisfied elegant couple. A well-mannered gentleman and lady are drinking coffee. A swallow and a glance at the street. A ragged Chinese speaks to them from outside [the window]. He pleads with them with his mouth and his eyes, with his eyebrows and his hands: not more than a few cents. And they, the couple—a swallow and glance . . . a swallow and a glance. . . . All three, the elegant

couple and the Chinese beggar leave the window together. The couple
to the taxi and the Chinese . . . ?

Fishman wrote three brief sketches, of which one is translated here, that
capture with few but sharp strokes the painful contrasts that met the
stranger in Shanghai. One sketch describes hungry Chinese children
dressed in rags, the other tells of a rickshaw puller who runs barefoot
at night in cold rain while his passenger sings. Brief though the "min-
iature" above is, it paints a powerful picture of the Shanghai scene and
the writer's revulsion at indifference to human suffering.

✳ YOSL MLOTEK ✳

A LETTER . . . (1943)[98]

A word, a word about me—I'll come for sure,
To me the great world's strange and tight.
Each night on firmaments I write
A fev'rish letter to you, "I long. . . . "

I mark with all the brightest stars
The most beautiful, tender song of faith.
And when you hear the rustling evening song—
Know, that it brings to you my greeting.

And if the sun will once neglect to shine,
Is barely seen through foggy clouds,
Know, that it was extinguished by the flames
Reflected in my longing dreams. . . .

A word, a word about me—I'll come for sure,
May storms carry me far like grains of sand.
In wandering I have found neither
Clarity nor true pleasure. . . .

In fev'rish nights I hear your name,
Your scorching tears my body burn.
Each wind whispers a reminder,
In every sound I hear your longing call.

☙

Mlotek's poem might strike us as banal, were it not for the fact that we
know where and under what circumstances he wrote it. Throughout the
poem he evoked the imagery of distance, of unreachability: writing letters

about heaven, stars, sunlessness, clouds, the unreality of dreams—all to express his sense of dissociation and displacement. Whereas dissociation is certainly in part the source of his anguish, it is not the message he wants most to convey. Rather, it is the affirmation in the thrice-repeated promise that he will send word, that he will return. Love, that precious gift, has not abandoned him; it continues to nourish his loneliness. And bearing this gift he will come back. The poet's thoughts were less for himself than for those whom he had left behind and from whom he was indefinitely separated.[99]

* YEHOSHUA RAPOPORT *

DIARY (excerpts, 1941–1943)[100]

May 12, 1941 (pp. 44–45)
I remember now my first meeting with Jewish Shanghai. Such a disappointment, such a blow to my hopes. . . . I had longed for even a small Jewish community where I can work again. When fate brought us to Shanghai, which was to be a solution to my spiritual imprisonment, I rejoiced: a city with a Jewish population! But the reception . . . was not what I expected. We arrived in the middle of the night after five hours at sea without warm food. The Jewish community in Shanghai did not receive the fifty refugees in their homes, but sent us to the Jewish Club, where we were to sit for the rest of the night. The rabbi did prepare a home for the rabbis and the rabbinic students, but for the writers and the simple Jews there was no place and we . . . were tossed into the Pingling shelter, into the pigsty, without a table, without a chair. . . . It was so hard to receive a few dollars for a flat—the local Jews regarded this with misgivings: why are we better than the German Jews [they asked]? They can live in the "Heime" [homes], and you cannot?

May 28, 1941 (pp. 46–47)
HICEM [the initials of the Jewish agencies Hias, Ica, Emig-Direkt—ed.] gave us the first month's rent. This was not that easy. But the second month's rent we had to receive from EastJewCom. . . . But that too is not that easily obtained. For this task a special person was selected . . . H. B.-R., a Jew, a rich man, who accumulated enormous wealth in dark deals, and owns whole streets in Hongkou. To him one must go and undergo an examination in order to receive fifteen dollars, or twenty Shanghai dollars per head. My conversation with him was brief but typical.

First, he does not speak Yiddish, Russian, or Polish. . . .

"How much do you pay?" he asks me.

"Eighty dollars."

"You have two rooms?" he asks and looks at me, quickly raising his eyes from the paper . . . like the investigating judge in a cheap criminal novel. I am thinking, he is well informed. And he is satisfied that he has caught a refugee at a crime—two rooms. I don't hesitate to tell him exactly how the rooms look so he should know how the Shanghai Jews have provided a Jewish writer and his family with a roof over his head.

June 2, 1941 (pp. 31–32)

I stood . . . and didn't know how to go to Albert Avenue and, as always this month, when I have to ask directions, I cannot stop wondering at how few Europeans one sees in the Settlement. To ask directions of a Chinese is useless, as I know from previous experience. First, they don't understand my question; second, I don't understand their answer. With my English it is difficult for me to communicate with a Jewish Englishman. . . . Finally I saw a face that was similar to a Jewish face. I approached him and asked in English. It turned out that he was going in the same direction. . . . After a few minutes, aware of my poor English, he asked if I speak Russian. I felt more at ease. One less torture. Now conversation was a little easier. But when he heard I am from Poland, he asked if I speak Yiddish. What a question! I grabbed it with both hands. Now my tongue became untied. My young man [he was only twenty-odd years old] spoke Yiddish quite well, considering the place and his age.

February 15, 1942 (pp. 36–39)

. . . One person judges the other. If one were able to judge oneself even if only with one tenth accuracy and objectivity, I would guarantee that the salvation of the world is near.

Another matter made me think . . . in the twenty years of my literary activity I did not have anything to do with such people [as E. Simkhoni and Jacob Fishman]. What had I in common with those who neither are gifted nor have a conscience . . . and no refinement? Now thrown into a corner of the world, separated from my environment and work, must I also be forced . . . to be connected with such . . . men and their petty pursuits . . . ?

It is good when in a city like Shanghai there are several Jewish writers. Perhaps, even if it is impossible to work "among the people," one could at least work in an intimate circle. One could work cooperatively, or could divide affairs among ourselves. Small lectures could be arranged, literary joys and sufferings could be shared.

But unfortunately the group of refugee writers from Poland is a fiction. . . . We, the Polish refugees, brought with us some who fit in the spiritual environment of Shanghai [this is meant ironically—ed.]. They are in the group of writers among the religious and among the assimilated. Ha, my luck; all my life I suffered from the Jewish "group epidemic" [that is, being assigned to a group—ed.], now it is also so in Shanghai. . . .

February 18, 1942 (pp. 69–70 [Rapoport crossed this entry out—ed.])
Cripples in the street . . . and their dead ones not buried (not even this last favor is for the Chinese poor). Once when I saw a driver sit in his rickshaw, waiting for a client, and reading meanwhile a newspaper or book, it occurred to me—at any rate, I feel this way—that Shanghai's Jewish wealth is more awful than Chinese poverty. Poverty here still has something spiritual about it, the will to rise, but Jewish wealth is only naked materialism, crude, with no attempt to reach for higher attainments . . . it is the lowest of the low.

undated entry (p. 73)
And when a person will have peace, contact with nature, pleasure from work (and not only nice work), enjoyment from art, perhaps he will be a much better person, one assumes. When it has needles in its skin, even the gentlest animal becomes wild.

March 15, 1943 (p. 267)
I told [Mordechai] Rotenberg and [Yosl] Mlotek that my intellectual labors are a kind of artificial respiration. It seems that they did understand this very well. I decided to write a book about Jewish Shanghai, and the chapter about my cultural work will be entitled "artificial respiration."

Mlotek is close to an intellectual crisis. This, in any event, one can infer from what he is saying, provided it is not a phase. He is certainly intelligent. He feels that here there is nothing with which to create a Jewish life, and he asks the tragic question: is it perhaps present and where might it be? This is precisely the misfortune . . . it has to be produced. No one prepared it for us.

April 30, 1943 (p. 287)
Today I submitted a request for a room in Hongkou. The mood—it is
normal at the moment. The worst is that I will again have to interrupt
work. This is already the third time in this war that I began again to
work, yet . . . work will not go forward. . . . It hurts so much. Work is my
element, or my drug, if you wish; without working I feel as if in a hostile
world because my own Jewish world—whether because of the Shanghai
Jews, or because of the refugees—is foreign to me, foreign, foreign.

July 16, 1943 (p. 338)
More than three hundred people who don't have an "allotment" and
don't have an "extension" must go today at once to Hongkou [in April
Rapoport received a three-month extension of his permission to remain
outside the ghetto—ed.]. . . . [July] 15 was supposed to be a meeting of
SACRA regarding this matter. . . . But the meeting was postponed because of Simkhoni's wedding.

Does one need better proof of who our Shanghai overactors are?

July 23, 1943 (pp. 346–47)
Again there is talk about an evacuation around October 1. And again I am
disturbed. An evacuation is so necessary . . . and there is so much insecurity about whether I am on the right list. What security can there be if it is
up to human beings to decide? Since I was not among the forty [people]
in the first evacuation, I cannot possibly be now either. Those who com-
pile the list will find a way to change names in favor of one or the other
person. The feeling of insecurity alone is the greatest anguish. [Such a
joke], I need to be uncertain about my place in an evacuation! Others
laugh at my insecurity, but I remember Vilna, where I was not offered an
opportunity to go to America, or Palestine, I was forgotten. . . . "

❧

Like Shoshana Kahan, Yehoshua Rapoport disliked Shanghai. But un-
like Kahan, who dreaded Shanghai even before she set foot in the city,
Rapoport was sorely disappointed by it. He had expected a flourishing
Jewish cultural life and instead found a pervasive vulgar materialism

among the Jewish nonrefugee population. He had hoped to find appreciation for his literary work and instead met with ignorance and even disdain. In crowded Shanghai he found no consideration for his need of a place to work. Indeed, in this kind of environment his own work seemed increasingly artificial and he thought of himself as being kept artificially alive. Time and again, together with others, he hoped to find his name on the evacuation list, yet each time he looked in vain. Writing the diary became for Rapoport a means to express his feelings of rejection and failure. He was profoundly unhappy and the diary provided the opportunity to express his secret longings, his dislike of many of his fellow refugees, and the desire for self-worth that was denied him, he felt, in Shanghai.

The two diaries represented in this book, the one by Kahan, the other by Rapoport, are very different. In part this is certainly due to the fact that Kahan's was edited and published, whereas Rapoport's has seemingly remained unedited and was never published. We might assume, therefore, that Rapoport's diary is more revealing of its author than Kahan's. A large part, however, must be ascribed to the self-perception of each individual. Although both belonged to the Jewish intelligentsia in Poland, one was a performer, the other a scholar. Where Kahan found considerable satisfaction in her Shanghai performances, Rapoport thought Shanghai Jewish intellectual life appalling, with Jewish learning, such as his, totally unappreciated.

Important, however, in the final analysis, is that the reader of another time and place can glimpse the immediate reaction of two very different kinds of people to the metropolis. Even if Rapoport confided to the diary very little about his family life and the hardships his wife and son no doubt endured, how he as an individual coped with cultural dislocation is clear. As readers we realize once again how important it is to consider exile an experience of individuals and not solely of groups.

＊ *ANONYMOUS* ＊

Time and distance do not yield this poet's identity. Indeed, "Szpilki, u mnie nie!" ("Pins, Not for Me") may have simply been written to blow off steam, and the writer may have been only an occasional contributor to *Echo Szanghajskie* (Shanghai echo).

PINS, NOT FOR ME (1944)[101]

In the course of the negotiations concerning the kitchen, a certain Mr. B who sat across in the temporary office of the mess hall let it be known that he will not move and will leave when he wants to leave.

> Not for me!
> Honorable Mr. B!
> That you're not permanent
> All refugees know.
> That you're here only now
> Could very well show
> That you're here out of spite.
> You'll get stuck with this needle, take fright.
>
> You want to remain?
> I can point the way.
> When we all leave
> You are welcome to stay.
>
> I should hope nothing bad
> Will result from this game
> Since I omit mentioning
> Your honorable name.

Those who write satire
Often choose to antagonize
When they don't want to
Persons, like you, Sir, immortalize.

I include this short poem here for two reasons. First, little attention has been paid in this collection so far to the non-Jewish Polish refugees in Shanghai, and their publication, *Echo Szanghajskie*, is virtually unknown. Stuck in Shanghai, far from their loved ones, their homeland occupied by a ruthless enemy, their future, should the war finally end, looked bleak indeed. A second reason is the attention to trivia, the petty annoyances that filled the lives of Shanghai refugees. This poem about a meaningless incident epitomizes what Lion Feuchtwanger has described as the life of exiles or expatriates: most often it consisted of small, unpleasant situations that were frequently quite ridiculous.[102]

* YONI FAYN *

(b. 1914)[103]

Yoni Fayn (also transliterated as Fain or Fein) was born in Kamienice-Podolskie, but moved to Vilna with his family as a young child and attended school there. In 1936 he went to Warsaw; he fled Poland in 1939, when Germany invaded the country. Together with the Polish group of intellectuals and writers, he ended up in Shanghai in 1941. Fayn left Shanghai for Mexico in 1947 and taught school there for the next nine years. In the year he arrived in Mexico, he published a volume of poetry, which includes several poems about Shanghai.[104] A year later, Diego Rivera, the well-known Mexican muralist, sponsored Fayn's one-man show in Mexico City. In 1956 Fayn left Mexico for New York, where he became professor of art at Hofstra University. Well known in Yiddish circles as both painter and poet, he has had several exhibitions of his paintings, and has continued to publish Yiddish poetry and prose, capturing in both media the spirit of an era. About Fayn's poetry Yehoshua Rapoport wrote that he has "excellent pictures, much thought, and deep feelings . . . [The poems are] written with head and soul, with heart, culture, and talent."[105] Described as "one of the last Yiddish-speaking expressionist artists," Fayn had an exhibit of his paintings at the London Jewish Cultural Center in October 2007 at the age of ninety-three.

☙

A POEM ABOUT SHANGHAI GHETTO (1945)[106]

Still one more song in simple rhyme
I'll sing for you today,
Not of mother's smile this song,
Nor of sails on rivers long.

For you I'll sing it quietly,
About how a ghetto in Shanghai,

Becomes like dust, can be gray,
Gray, like dust can be in May.

Great is Shanghai, lawless and wild,
Full of bodies, wind, and mice,
Full of talk, falling heavy,
Full of tears—white like rice.
A hundred nations thrown together
Are rotting on its wet terrain,
Greed and gold intermingle,
Wiped out by the rain.

But Japan wants to discover
The Jewish tribe at Huangpu River,
Threefold service for the Jew,
Japan's sun's rising large and new.

Once there was a Chinese wall,
A Jewish wall should stand instead,
Japan too needs a city of sorrow,
Familiar from Europe to borrow.
Among the ruins
Jews are herded about,
Bundles lie as night falls,
Left behind from Egypt's rout.
Bent over old Jews sit,
Crawl like clouds dark red,
To look with old, tired eyes
In refuse for a piece of bread.

Winds blow from the Yellow Sea,
Trees sway and swing,
Flames shake and tremble,
Night flies hum and sing.

And the wind's already gone,
In the darkness children shriek,

Hidden corners harbor dread,
Doors when locked noisily creak.

By the wind a new day's brought,
In the street queues wait,
Human beings are not dogs
For passes written at the gate.
Ghoya's great, he gives the pass,
The Jew obediently bows:
"Honor to Japan, her might,
Soon to rival our plight!"
Ghoya smiles: I am a king,
Shanghai's king of Jews,
The wanderers smile submissively,
A king beats up anyone he'll choose.

There in Europe ascends the stairs
Holding a rope a second king,
Counting the dead children's heads
He cries, his luck has lost its sting.
His name's no longer mentioned,
Remembered he is no more.
Quietly from mirrors he steps to,
Asking himself: who are you?
Are you the messiah, master of Jews,
The king that spiders have led?
He looks about, he's pale and thin,
And goes on to be with the dead.

But here in far away China land,
One Ghoya only for the Jewish race,
King of pain, king of shame,
Glory to you, king, peace and praise.
All being's a game, after all,
Games with filth, games with heaven,
Stone and dust, blood and wine,

White tears and yellow mold.
Today you are, on another day
This one takes men, the other money.
Games of duties, games of worry,
Games of guns and fans.
A crooked back suits the game,
Better yet a blind eye,
A floor's well swept with a head of hair,
A larger broom of several heads a worthy try.

Games for the small ones, praising flies,
Praising crumbs, also decay.
What for the joy of victories,
What for great power, say?
What for, what for the God of Jews
Better a god of flies.
King Ghoya in the ghetto walks,
Hits people and stamps passes twice.

Old games, circle of pranksters!
Let me be the last transiteer,
Taking the last shaky stride,
And having the first eye without a tear.

Shanghai ghetto, land of Jews
Your citizenship I gladly take,
Let it be my hand, a beggar's hand,
My yellow pass shall be my flag.
I'll stand in the long queue
To receive blows on my face,
Plead for bread because I hurt
Smiling, beg for your grace.

Only at late midnight hour,
Dark sayings will I plant,

Because I fell I now can dare
To carry death in merriment.
Be forgotten, dear brother,
Be forgotten, also love,
The tenderness of high fever,
No longer am I tough.
Cursed be the hour of rest,
Pursued by murderers everywhere,
Let me hate like you,
Hiding my bloodied money from your stare.

No more days of free believing,
The murdered body's cut I'll be,
Or be the child collecting contributions,
Or as the murderer's wife stand in the alley.

No more sunny songs,
Here's a song my blood demands.
No more words, brothers,
Only persons, weak ones, are friends.
No longer do I want to be weak,
Night, to my prayer pay heed,
Here speaks your son, an anguished man,
Here speaks a Jewish poet in need.

This is the end, blind night,
Take it, like circling and cawing crows,
The ghetto mumbles, wakes up,
Eagerly striding, I walk as one who perhaps knows.

The bitterness in this poem is palpable, a sharp contrast to Simkhoni's poem, "Three Countries Spat Me Out." Among Shanghai poems, this is a unique attempt to incorporate the condition of the Shanghai survivors into the context of Jewish history, encompassing the Egyptian past, the European present, as well as the Shanghai war years. Fayn's images are both personal and general. They are from the ghetto and from the slaughter of Jews in Europe. The notorious Kanoh Ghoya (see fig. 10, above), the subject of the poem by Herbert Zernik (below), has a role in Fayn's poem as well; Ghoya, the king of Jews who signs passes and arbitrarily beats up the ghetto Jews. Hitler, too, seems to put in an appearance as the "second king" who is already dead. There is a brief mention of Japan, but this is not a political poem, and the few references at the beginning are not repeated. Blood, murder and murderers, hate, fear, hunger, darkness—these are the words that recur time and again, as if the poet were caught in a nightmare from which he cannot escape. His anguish is a game, a disgusting, unreal, never-ending game of unspeakable cruelty.

Yet, Fayn is not after the search for the real, asking what existence is all about, asking for hope or a release of some sort. Rather, he is caught in a torment from which there is no reprieve and in which even the God of the Jews is powerless. This being so, the poet seems to say that to go on living is to face the cruelty, murder, and ugliness all around, including one's own weakness and inability to change things. The last phrase is revealing, "as one who perhaps knows." Fayn does not pretend to utter certainties. For if everything having to do with existence is a game, there can be only one certainty, namely that a game is taking place and no more. Like Zernik, Fayn quite likely penned these verses after the end of war, when it was safe to write poems exposing Ghoya and Japan's ambitions.

* HERBERT ZERNIK *

(1903–1972?)

Herbert Zernik began his acting career at the age of sixteen in Berlin, playing mostly comic roles. He was incarcerated in Buchenwald for a time, and, upon being released, went to Shanghai, where he continued a successful acting career. After World War II, he lived briefly in the United States and later returned to Germany.

A MONKEY TURNED HUMAN (1945)[107]

A zoo was somewhere in this world
at a special spot for its beauty renown'd.
Admired by all,
it had zebras and bears that were brown.
But the greatest attraction of all
was the miraculous monkey "Go"
whom everyone knew.
He cycles, makes music, eats, drinks,
Indeed, our well-trained monkey also thinks.
Alone, quietly on his tree
he sat, dreaming and wishing
for once to be like those outside the fence,
no longer a monkey, a person perchance.
Biding his time until a door was left open,
too late it was realized
that Go had departed.
High and low went the search,
the miraculous monkey had left his perch.
He put on a suit, a haircut came next,
now Go seemed so tame
and English he spoke,

revenge on mankind was his aim.
A town full of dispossessed people,
he chose to carry out his evil
intentions.
They called him "Sir," he reigned like a king,
furnished an office with a "scream" table
and ruled his subjects most capable.
But if one came along
who treated him wrong
he rolled his eyes, gasped for air
and yelled, "I'll shoot you, you liar."
Then came the toadies, gentlemen of rank
who led him from one celebration to another.
Though he was universally hated,
the gentlemen seemed much elated.
Monkeys like men,
he laughed to himself.
Pretending to be musically smart ·
he was also a critic of art
and scratched on the violin,
which the toadies declared bewitchin'.
In his megalomania
he invented an "order" in pink and blue
for people to wear.
To his stupid questions he demanded an answer.
People stood for hours waiting for him
until he dismissed them on a whim.
The cultured and the low
had to bow
when he strutted through town.
And if someone missed a greeting
he would receive a beating.
More impudent and bold each day
until revenge was on the way,
found by the zoo's keeper
he was grabbed and put where he should be

high on the tree.
There he sits grinding his teeth, dreaming his dream
again a monkey—he always was and forever will be
undressed as before
the party's no more.

Kanoh Ghoya, the subject of Zernik's poem, was a man hated by one and all. According to all accounts, he was sadistic and brutal, and he arbitrarily used his power to issue passes to leave Hongkou. Zernik's poem, probably written as soon as the war ended, expressed the sentiments of most, if not all, ghetto inhabitants, who feared this man, yet had no choice but to endure his abuse if they wanted to leave Hongkou.

✳ SHOSHANA KAHAN ✳

(ROSE SHOSHANA KAHAN, 1895–1968)[108]
Born in Lódz, Shoshana Kahan (fig. 17) was orphaned at an early age. She was best known as an actress of the Yiddish stage, but she was also a skillful translator of drama and the author of poems and a number of novels. These appeared in Lithuania, Argentina, and elsewhere, often under pen names. Shoshana Kahan was married to Leyzer Kahan (1885–1946), also a writer, and both fled to Vilna when the Germans marched into Poland. They reached Shanghai in 1941 together with the group of Polish-Jewish writers. Her diary is valuable because large portions were written during the years of her exile and reflect not only her own feelings but those of many, if not most, of her fellow Polish refugees. To be recipients of charity in Shanghai, charity not willingly given, the Poles felt, was an added punishment to that of homelessness. After a brilliant performance of *Mirele Efros* on May 5, 1946,[109] both she and

her husband became ill with typhus fever. Leyzer died some weeks later. Shoshana recovered and left Shanghai in 1946 for New York, where she continued her writing career and where several of her novels were adapted for the Yiddish stage.

✿

17. Shoshana Kahan. From *Leksikon fun yidishn teater* (Lexicon of the Yiddish theater), ed. Zalmen Zylbercwajg, Vol. 3 (New York: Elisheva, 1959).

IN FIRE AND FLAMES: DIARY OF A JEWISH ACTRESS (excerpts, 1941–1945)[110]

October 10, 1941 (pp. 278–79)
We will have to go to Shanghai, even if terrible letters arrive from there. The transit visas are no longer extended for remaining here [in Kobe].

Today a large group left. A strong war atmosphere prevails. Again we are sitting in the dark, again we run to see if our names are on the list to leave. Before, when a person saw his name on the departure list, he was happy. Today, when he sees that he is on the list for Shanghai, he cries.

October 25, 1941 (p. 282)
Arrived in Shanghai on the 23rd. All our friends were waiting at the port with flowers. When we were still on the ship one could see the enormous contrast with the Japanese. The Japanese work diligently and quietly, the Chinese, slowly and very noisily. You never hear his [the Chinese] steps because he wears soft slippers and straw sandals, but you always hear his yelling. Whether they carry a small or a heavy burden, they always sing "Eho, Eho." One Chinese wants to deprive another of his income, and immediately fifteen Chinese come running. . . . Everybody grabbed a piece of [our] luggage and I was simply scared. . . .

December 8, 1941 (p. 289)
What will be now? We are again in the fire of war. God in heaven, haven't we suffered enough? The Pacific War between Japan and the United States began today in the morning. No longer can one find a piece of earth in God's world where there is peace. All our friends are running around like poisoned mice. . . . The last hope has disappeared, [we are] without any help. Until now we still received a few pennies from the Joint [Distribution Committee]. Since Miss Margolis came from the Joint, the situation for the refugees had become altogether a little easier. EastJewCom had, moreover, taken over the administration of the Polish and Lithuanian Jews, and we no longer had dealings with the Speelman Committee. EastJewCom was in contact with the Joint, and now it will no longer be possible to receive money from abroad. Abandoned in an Asian country, who knows what will happen to us now? . . .

March 8, 1942 (p. 291)
I am not afraid of working hard, and already today we gave a performance for Purim. This time it was a variety show, *Homentashen with Rice* [homentashen are triangular pastries customarily filled with poppy

seeds—ed.], a name we gave to today's performance in accordance with Shanghai fashion.

The writer Moyshe Elboym wrote the various numbers, the sketches as well as the songs were written by Svislacki and Markus, and the famous professor of music, Shaynboym, wrote the music. Leyzer Kahan was the literary manager. The theater was sold out. But not much will remain [for salaries]. I am no longer receiving support from EastJewCom—they are saying that I already "earn" on my own—but I am glad that we are giving the Shanghai Jews the opportunity to hear a Yiddish word. Many numbers were forbidden by the Japanese authority, among them the major number, "A Journey Around the World," by D. Markus.

April 16, 1942 (p. 292)

Leyzer came home today in a good mood. Together with the writers' delegation, he went to see Ambassador [Tadeusz] Romer, who also had to leave Japan for Shanghai. The ambassador explained that the evacuation questions [Polish citizens were able to leave Shanghai for other countries if their names appeared on the list—ed.] look very positive, and writers, who are more endangered than other refugees, will be evacuated to another country for their own safety. This means that there is hope to be saved from Shanghai . . . my God, may we not be disappointed this time.

May 10, 1942 (pp. 292–93)

Today was the opening of *Tevye the Dairyman,* and I played Golda. I had to resign from the variety show, first because in Shanghai we could not find enough variety show talent. In Shanghai, moreover, one can present a performance only once because there is no audience for a second performance. The show was also so expensive that even a sold-out house did not cover the costs. Closing the variety show was the only way out, and a return to plays, specifically Yiddish plays. But where to find texts?

I sat down with my husband Leyzer's help and wrote from memory Sholem Aleichem's *Tevye the Dairyman,* which I had performed with Morris Lampe hundreds of times before in Europe.

I also knew where able amateurs lived. I had to go to their homes to teach them their parts in Yiddish. By myself I created theater properties, direct the plays, and perform in them. But I derive great pleasure because of the sold-out performances, not only for material reasons but also because of the artistic success.

July 20, 1942 (p. 294)

I am still in the hospital, but I feel a lot better. Today [a rumor] can be heard that all the refugees will be sent to a concentration camp.

A few days ago there was an official notification regarding the evacuation of British citizens and together with them also Polish ones. Everyone's heart is beating faster: whom will the Polish ambassador take along . . . ? Fifty places are assigned to Polish citizens. Clearly, the few Christian refugees will be in the first place; then the converts; the famous assimilationists; only thereafter the other refugees. And there are [no more than] fifty places altogether.

July 25, 1942 (pp. 294–95)

I feel worse again. Leyzer goes about like a shadow. It is already known who is on the evacuation list. His name is not on the list. Despite the fact that he is the president of the writers' group and despite the fact that the Polish ambassador has promised that the writers will be the first to leave because they are more endangered. Despite all this, not a single writer is on the list. [Romer] is angry at the writers who confront with dignity the attempt to force them to accept the rules of a few assimilated Jews. . . . Meanwhile people come to the hospital to wish me good luck, saying to the doctor that he must see to it that I get up from bed because I am going away . . . poor Leyzer, again disappointed, again losing hope.

February 18, 1943 (pp. 298–99)

What we feared has finally happened. Today the official proclamation appeared that everyone who came after 1937 must move into a special neighborhood. It is called by the polite [name] "permitted district" [designated area]; one is ashamed to call it by its real name, "ghetto." In truth, we will be locked inside a ghetto. And for this we had to run thousands of miles in order to fall into a ghetto here.

Recently, times have been hard for the refugees. Real hunger is prevalent. Almost all people now have blisters on their tongue due to vitamin deficiency, and the prescription that the refugee doctor Steinman gave was for one egg each day. The nice, idealistic doctor Steinman had to battle a lot until he agreed to the one egg.

Leyzer has also red gums and a red tongue. He is eating yeast [to counteract] the lack of vitamins. Everyone is walking around gloomy. They have given us until May 18 to move, three months.

March 30, 1943 (pp. 299–300)
A terrible situation. SACRA [Shanghai Ashkenazi Collaborating Relief Association] (a committee established by the Japanese and consisting of rich residents who are required to move the refugees into the ghetto) announced in the newspaper several days ago that the Polish refugees must register because they [too] must go into the ghetto. SACRA is hated by all the refugees because the refugees believe that SACRA should not have accepted the ugly task of helping to push us into the ghetto. It is understandable that the announcement in the newspaper has angered the Polish refugees. There are meetings and consultations on how to avoid the ghetto, with the majority of the refugees thinking that it is better to send us to concentration camps, as was done with the English and Americans, and to declare us enemies, instead of sending us into a ghetto. Many think [however] that a ghetto is better than a camp[, a view with which] the rich Jews side. But the help that they [the rich Jews] give us we could have done without. . . .

Today EastJewCom locked the [soup] kitchen because the refugees are meeting there about not going into the ghetto. When Leyzer came as usual with the pot to get a little rice he found the kitchen closed. And so the hungry refugees stood with their pots in front of the kitchen that they themselves had established with only a small sum from EastJewCom. We are being punished by not being given food to eat. An awful fuss developed. In the last few days there have been constant scandals because [people's] tempers are boiling over.

May 18, 1943 (pp. 301–302)
Today was a huge scandal in SACRA with the yeshiva students, all because of the ghetto and because of the scarcity of rooms. The students had demolished [the place and] thirty-three of the Yeshiva students were arrested. The sadists prepared for them the "Salweishan," a

camp for Chinese hooligans—thieves and criminals who were released from jail.

The yeshiva students were opposed to this and didn't want to go there. They insisted that they will rent apartments with their own money because they must study and cannot sit in such a dreadful house. It didn't help. The Japanese murderers did not want to withdraw their demand and the order was not changed. Therefore the yeshiva students went to SACRA, whose job it is to move the refugees into the ghetto. [In SACRA] sat the bandit Tsutomu Kubota very calmly . . . surrounded by the Jews who were quivering before him.

The yeshiva students staged a revolution, they broke everything they found, and the wealthy [Jewish] inhabitants spared no money and effort to suppress the story. With the help of the "revolution," the students did not go to Salweishan. The [Jewish] inhabitants prevailed upon the bandit Kubota to allow them to rent apartments at their own expense.

The students were the heroes of the day. All Shanghai talked about the "revolutionaries."

September 11, 1943 (p. 303)
Lilke, my daughter, sent a telegram from the Vatican. She wrote that she is in the Vatican. Now I need not worry about her. She prepaid the answer, but telegrams to Italy are not accepted [by the post office].

April 20, 1944 (p. 309)
This being packed together is awful. At night we open the door and put up the folding bed, [which now juts out] halfway into the hallway. Tonight was an "alarm" because of air raid exercises and the upstairs neighbors could not run fast enough downstairs because our bed was standing next to the stairs and it took a few minutes to fold up the bed. A few refugees were arrested. [But] Engelman and Bolek Silberberg were released today. They were arrested when they did not come into the ghetto on time. Rip and Y. Rapoport were also arrested for the same offense. Now a new group of latecomer refugees are going to Okura to register.

August 15, 1944 (pp. 319–20)
Leyzer is still in the hospital and does not feel well. The heat is killing [me] and I did not get a pass to visit him. But I received a pass to go to the

club [which was in the International Settlement]. Well, I learned how to smuggle myself with this pass into the French Concession. Today, of all times, was a streetcar inspection and I was a bit scared, but the Japanese did not go near the women, and we went on. I got away with only a fright. The city is boiling, all those who arrived after 1937 must register. Residents and all refugees who have extensions and exemptions must register. Even residents wait [now] for bad edicts. There is talk that for us, the refugees from the ghetto, places are prepared on an island and [after we leave] the residents will come to the ghetto in our place.

November 21, 1944 (p. 325)
A terrible day and a terrible night. The air raid alarms and bombardments go on the whole night and the whole day. Bombs have fallen on the Japanese area of Yangzipu. Trucks and cars full of wounded people are going by. Hospitals are full with wounded Chinese. . . .

December 10, 1944 (pp. 326–27)
With luck I have become a merchant. It is very hard, and many a "madam" regards me with disdain, but that is how it is. One has to participate in the dance. Leyzer does not feel well, he must have better nourishment. . . . Since bombs started falling, it has become impossible to buy anything. People want to have some provisions at home. So I have taken to dealing. To arrange performances in the ghetto is impossible. Most of the refugees are from Germany and Austria and don't understand Yiddish. There are only about eight hundred Polish refugees, most of them yeshiva students; there is simply no audience here. . . .

December 20, 1944 (p. 327)
I earn quite well dealing, but today I did not go to the city [the International Settlement]. My feet hurt from having to climb many stories. In order to sell a small bottle of oil one has to go way up; everybody lives up high. Yesterday I was on the eighth floor at Madam Panivishki's three times. She is a good client and I wanted to earn money. Twice I was at Bitker's apartment on the ninth floor to take the order and deliver the merchandise. If nobody had been at home, I would have had to go a third time to get paid. When I went home yesterday in the rain I cried all the way.

July 18, 1945 (pp. 338–40)

People had not yet calmed down from last night's bombardment, when a heavy attack occurred again today. After it stopped, trucks with the wounded began once more to roll. This time the bombs fell on the [International] Settlement and Nantao. Yesterday's devastation was terrible. Hundreds of people were killed, among them forty Jews. Thousands were wounded yesterday and thousands more today. Celmeister's daughter, Ruth Wilner, died; the young Kushnir died; the second young Kushnir was severely wounded; the children of the Bundist [meaning that he belonged to the socialist party], Berl Amberos, were wounded. The Jewish doctors work day and night, bandaging and operating. . . . Without medicines and without instruments they perform operations with plain knives. The refugees work with superhuman strength to save those who are buried in the ruins. Everyone is very upset that the Americans bombed the ghetto.

Now we have the funerals of the Polish [refugees] that were killed. All of us came to the Ward Road synagogue. The yeshiva students and rabbis came, many residents, friends of the refugees, the Rabbis Ashkenazi and Hayim. . . . When Rabbi Levensohn . . . and Yoni Fayn spoke, heartrending weeping was heard.

The heat was terrible. Awful lamentations began when the trucks with the dead bodies arrived. They were covered with bloody rags and swarms of flies crawled on the bodies, on which the blood had dried. The trucks had left the synagogue quickly because the bodies were already becoming bloated. Mrs. Kushnir was given an injection before going to the cemetery, [and as a result] she had absolutely no idea what was happening. When her husband and son were lowered into the double grave, the poor woman watched it as if it had no connection with her. People wept uncontrollably and the woman just stood there nonchalantly, not aware of her misfortune. Tired and brokenhearted we returned from the cemetery. We talked about the poor . . . [man] who had been in the [refugee] kitchen to fetch food for himself, his wife, and daughter. Everyone had warned him to wait until the bombing attack was over and then go. But the man said that his poor wife, who works so hard, came from the city hungry and tired; he will quickly run home with the food. He never got home. . . . Body parts that were his were found not far from the kitchen, scattered about in various places together with the soup from the refugee kitchen, the pot still standing at the side. Aygla, the erstwhile rich man from Białystok, had been unable to get a special pass. But his wife, Khava, an energetic woman used to every comfort in life, did get a special pass and went every day to the city to do business. She dragged several pounds of sugar to rich people; sold wine for the holidays; crept up tens of flights of stairs each day in order to feed her family. He, Boris Aygla, stood every noon in line in freezing cold and boiling heat. He took the place of his wife, who every ten days had to renew her special pass. He always felt bad because his wife worked and not he. He wanted to help at least at home as much as possible and he always brought dinner from the refugee kitchen . . . where death found him. . . . When we got home from the cemetery we [again] heard heavy shooting. People started running not knowing where to go. The Chinese panicked. Only later did we find out that [the noise] had been thunder, a storm, a typhoon, and downpour, and we were glad. Airplanes will not fly [in this weather].

August 11, 1945 (p. 346)
[Word comes at night while she was visiting friends outside the ghetto that the war has ended—ed.] We could not sleep. We got up, dressed, and went out into the street to find a newspaper. Much movement in the street . . . strangers are kissing one another, congratulating each other, Chinese, Russians, like one family. An official announcement of peace is not in the newspaper, only that Japan has capitulated and that the imperial family will remain in power. Still, the joy is great and nobody is asking for details. We are drunk with the word "peace." We dreamt about it while asleep, thought about it while awake, breathed "peace," and now I hear the word everywhere. How good it is to hear the word.

October 30, 1945 (p. 359)
This morning we were informed that a telegram has arrived for us at HICEM [the initials of the Jewish agencies Hias, Ica, Emig-Direkt—ed.]. Leyzer immediately rushed into the city, waiting for the office to open. The telegram is from the Vatican. It tells us that Lili [the Kahans' daughter] is in good health. She has received our letter and has also answered it. [The telegram] was signed by the Vatican secretary. Does this

mean that my child was in danger and had to hide in the Vatican . . . why else would the Vatican secretary sign the telegram and not she alone? Might she be under arrest? One's head can explode thinking. . . . Leyzer left soon to send a telegram to Lili and to our cousin George to send us affidavits. Now we work only for the postal services, as soon as we have a little money we send letters and telegrams. If only they would bring us replies.

December 16, 1945 (pp. 365–66)
The Mir Yeshiva has posted a list of Jews who were saved in Warsaw. We all besieged the house of the yeshiva. Everybody pushed to take a look, perhaps he will [find] one of his near ones. Many refugees didn't want to go close to the list, they don't want to know the truth that they don't have anyone anymore. . . . I read. A jubilant scream is torn from my breast: I have found a name, Jonas Turkov and his wife, Diana Blumenfeld.[111] They were saved. As I read on under "K" my heart begins to beat faster when I see the name of Samuel Kahan: my son's name. But I soon see that this Samuel Kahan is seventy years old; he should live and be healthy, he surely has children who will be happy to see his name. But this is not my son. I soon sent a telegram with greetings, asking to discover [something] about my children. I sent letters and telegrams to all acquaintances, near and far in every country and city, but regrettably until now I have received no replies, not even to the telegrams.

Although the last third of the diary was edited,[112] thus leaving only around one hundred pages for Shanghai, the diary is an extremely valuable contribution to works about wartime Shanghai. Kahan began keeping a record from the first week of World War II in September 1939, describing in detail the departure of her husband, Leyzer, her sons, and eventually of herself from Warsaw. There is the flight to Vilna, where she was reunited with her husband, the journey to Moscow, and the trip on the Trans-Siberian railway to Vladivostok. From Vladivostok the group of Polish-Jewish writers, together with others, traveled to Kobe and, eight months later, to Shanghai. They had been received warmly by the

Russian-Jewish community in Kobe; they liked the city, the friendliness of the Japanese population, and they dreaded the news they were receiving about conditions in Shanghai.

As it turned out, life was indeed very harsh there. Kahan mentions frequently how she and the other Polish refugees resisted sharing the fate of the German and Austrian exiles who lived in crowded dormitories. As long as the American Joint Distribution Committee (JDC, "Joint" in her diary) sent money to Shanghai toward the refugees' support, the situation was bearable. The Committee for Assistance of Jewish Refugees from Eastern Europe (EastJewCom), organized in March 1941, much to the relief of the Polish group, had assumed responsibility for their care. But the Pacific War changed all this for the worse when the JDC money no longer reached Shanghai. In February 1943 came another blow when all stateless Jews who had come to Shanghai after 1937, including the Polish group, had to move into a small area of Hongkou, the ghetto, called euphemistically the "designated area." Kahan describes in graphic detail the rebellious Polish group whose resistance to moving into the ghetto in 1943 did not, however, help them.

Despite the new hardships caused by the air strike alarms, the refugees were glad to see American bombers over Shanghai, for it meant that the war's end was near. But then occurred the catastrophe of July 1945, when American bombs also fell on Hongkou. Kahan lets us understand how this air strike affected the lives of individuals and families. Through her eyes we see the moving scene at the cemetery where the mourners assembled, and hear the conversations about the man who was killed fetching food for his family.

At the end of war, in 1945, began the frantic search for relatives who may have survived the cataclysm. Her moving description about reading lists of names, or the futile wait for a letter, are unforgettable. The picture she paints of people pushing one another to read the lists occurred not only in Shanghai, but wherever Jews congregated in Europe. There were the many sad and tearstained faces and the few people who rejoiced upon finding a familiar name. In the summer of 1946 both she and her husband came down with a very severe case of typhus. Leyzer Kahan succumbed to the disease and passed away in June 1946. Shoshana wrote movingly in her diary on July 12:

A black page. A sad one. Leyzer is no more. My husband is no more. . . . I was not even at his funeral, I was not even at his sickbed. He died alone, forsaken . . . alone like a stone . . . neither a child nor the wife accompanied him to his eternal rest, did not hear his last wish. (p. 381)

The diary concludes with her departure from Shanghai for the United States in October 1946.

Diaries from this period are extremely scarce. What makes Kahan's diary uniquely important are her observations of the small details of everyday life, generally not noted by historians. Not the world's events, but how to find food, the success of her performance in the Jewish Club, how to cope with illness, how to make a living—these are the topics that preoccupy her. The diary allows us a small glimpse into the life of one woman and her attempt to preserve her humanity under the harsh conditions of war and exile.

* KURT LEWIN *

After World War's bloody battle,
Calmer times have come our way,
And I say, though not too subtle,
Rather boring is the day.
Not a victory, not a hero,
Nothing new, I won't pretend,
Here is something less than zero
For a salad of this weekend.
Ibn Saud, he's not moving,
Strikers' strikes are calmly ended,
Nuremberg trial's slowly proving
That great crimes can still be mended.
The globe is filled with wreaths of peace,
Of conferences there's no decrease,
Peace is here—'tis our creed,
Let's build bigger bombs indeed.
Water from the trusty line
Is now salty, says the news,
UNRRA pills, I hence opine
Will kill salts without abuse.
If the chlorine is too sticky,
Chemists, it's your duty's aim,
To invent a pill less icky,
That succeeds without more waste
To suppress the chlorine taste.
Meanwhile city's high authority
Wants to widen our lane,
So that we'll walk more easily
On the Bund even in rain.
Thus quite well digestible,

Everything's prepared on hand,
For a salad of week's end.
We are ready, this I mean,
Yours sincerely,
Kurt Lewin

"Der Wochensalat" (The weekly salad) became a regular feature in the *Shanghai Herald*, and Lewin masterfully combines in this poem both foreign and Shanghai events. The trial of German war criminals held at Nuremberg is juxtaposed to the Cold War passion of building atom bombs. He ridicules the United Nations Refugee Relief Association's panacea of pills to clean the drinking water and juxtaposes this to a walk along the fashionable Bund, the well-known avenue of banks and foreign businesses along the Huangpu River. Lewin's satiric poems are among the best poems written in exile, and he continued to write these even after the war ended. In part, no doubt, it was his mastery of language, in both prose and poetry, that allowed Lewin to return to Germany instead of attempting to emigrate elsewhere, as did most of the Shanghai refugees.

Noteworthy as well is the tendency of these German poets to write satiric poems (though other poetry was also written), as reflected in the Karl Heinz Wolff and Herbert Zernik poems translated above. In contrast, the Yiddish poets did not resort to this literary device. Satirizing exile, according to Werner Vordtriede, should not be considered peripheral joking or ridicule. It is a major part of exile literature, a weapon against the spoilers of tradition in their native countries and a corrective while involuntarily abroad.[114]

* *JACOB H. FISHMAN* *

A WEDDING (1947)[115]
Despite the severely pointed mustache and the soldierly click of his
shoes, Robert Stein had the face of a defeated man. His mustache and
the soldierly click of his shoes, like the picture on the wall, described a
serious military man, remnants of a time gone by. Once all these had
a value, but not today, which is the reason why he looked so unhappy.
One can understand it. Still, even one year before the war, Robert Stein
deluded himself that he was Germany's eternal citizen, and his Aryan
merchant friends had given him no hints of anti-Semitism. Nice relationships. Therefore, he did not believe his eyes when he saw the announcement from the police that he and his family must leave Germany
within eight days. At that time he dashed from office to office in search
of an explanation until he became convinced that, alas, it was not a mis-
take. It was an unfortunate disaster.

During the entire journey from Berlin to Shanghai, Robert Stein felt
ashamed in front of his two children. Kurt was a youngster of fifteen
years and a real German boy: tall, blond, and proud. Elsa was two years
younger than her brother; she resembled him and was also tall and
blond, but with one difference: she was sad and clung to her mother.
Robert felt ashamed, like someone who convinced a friend about a matter that was to bring him good fortune and in the end caused him a great
misfortune. It seemed to Robert that the two children would learn now
that they were Jews. He did not want to think of that, yet it thought itself
quite without his intending to.

. . . .

At first Robert Stein imagined that once they came to Shanghai everything would be all right. He assured Grete, his wife, and the children
that the bad times would soon end, the war too would be over soon, and
the "gang of pigs," as he called Hitler and his clique, would be defeated.
Then everyone will return home. But matters developed differently and
more misfortunes followed . . . because the main principle of the de-

velopment was in Shanghai. The Japanese, the occupiers of Shanghai, were preparing a ghetto for the newly arrived European Jews. Bad luck followed them.

Robert did what all the others did. He gathered up their belongings and moved into the ghetto. Grete and Elsa went with him, but Kurt refused. A boy like an oak, with a German non-Jewish face, and eyes of a rapacious bird, he announced to his parents that he was not going. He was not about to be locked up in a ghetto. How will he avoid it? Not to worry, he will get papers. Robert considered preparing illegal papers scandalous, but he was ashamed that his son was more ingenious than he.

. . . .

Robert's dream of starting anew and engaging in business dissolved in the ghetto. Robert Stein, the erstwhile Berlin merchant and German military man, went with a metal pot to the barrack kitchen where it was filled with various foods mixed together. "Awful," mumbled Robert angrily and went home with the pot. When Grete lifted the lid and saw the disgusting stew she felt faint and scolded, "What the blazes!" [*Donnerwetter*].

Kurt came once a week from the city and brought some fruit for his parents and Elsa. He was proud of himself; he was not in the ghetto, had money in his pockets, and helped his parents and sister. Kurt told them strange stories about his good fortune and, even though his father didn't want to hear about these things, he ate the apples like a hungry man, as did Kurt's mother and Elsa. After another of their nauseating noon meals a little fruit was a pleasure and good for one's health. They praised the food while eating: "Wonderful!"

. . . .

Each day, after helping her mother with the chores, Elsa went to the Broyde family, who lived in the same lane. She often remained there until late at night, being attracted to the family despite the fact that the Broydes were Polish Jews and Mr. Broyde was a rabbi. Elsa felt at home there as if they were her family.

It was always lively at their home, full of people who had come to visit. They were mostly refugees, even young yeshiva students. All felt at home. Malkele, Mrs. Broyde, was so happy with everyone as if she were grateful that they had come. She was even happier when some kind of work was brought along. Her two-year-old son, Mendele, was a delightfully bright child who never cried. On the contrary, he always sang. He went to everybody, hugging everyone, jumping on their hands and shoulders. Because of little Mendele, Elsa felt at home at the Broydes. She had seen the child for the first time in the lane when he pulled her over with his small hands. Mrs. Broyde was happy that Mendele had become fond of Robert Stein's blond daughter. This is why Elsa began to go over to the Broyde family. In the beginning she went there for only an hour, but a day later she remained at the Broydes' longer. She felt good there. She didn't feel like leaving. She felt an attachment not only to Mendele, but also to the Broydes and to all the people she met at their home. This situation was, however, not to her father's liking; to what purpose must she crawl to these Polish Jews, especially to a rabbi? Her mother's exclamation, "What the blazes!" was of no help.

. . . .

In the city Kurt was busy all day long wheeling and dealing. Wherever a deal was to be made, Kurt made sure to participate in it, to get part of the earnings, and to have money to spend. He ate in the largest restaurants, ordered only the choicest dishes, fat dribbling from his mouth. Only the day before, Kurt had taken his Chinese neighbor's daughter, Luo Zhen, to a restaurant, ordering the most expensive food and drink on the menu for her, food she had not imagined in her wildest dreams. Kurt did not declare his love; he did not woo her with pretty words. After all, what kind of talk could there be between the two, him not knowing Chinese and she not a word of German? But she was taken by his appearance: a boy like an oak glancing about himself authoritatively. She looked at him with her trusting childish eyes. Her eyes caressed him as if they wanted to cling to the giant boy, for she found in Kurt much gentleness. He did not spare money on her; she should dress nicely and eat well.

Luo Zhen's father was a poor carpenter who worked in the lane from early morning until late at night, cutting boards and planing them without being aware that he had a grown-up daughter. He was completely oblivious to the fact that Luo Zhen was a graceful and good-looking girl for whom he should arrange a marriage. All he did all day long until late at night was cut boards and plane them. Once, however, the poor carpenter noticed a "nokenyo" (a white man, a foreigner) near his girl, and he almost lost his mind. He had a very low opinion of foreigners. Like a madman he ran to his wife, though she was unable to understand what he was asking. She looked at him as if he were a half-wit. So he decided to confront Luo Zhen himself, demanding that she tell the truth. Thus did he learn for the first time that she and Kurt, who lived in the lane, were in love and that Kurt was a good boy. She loved him. That was all.

At mealtime the carpenter said to his wife that the only solution was a wedding. Once the nokenyo was married to Luo Zhen, he, the carpenter, would be quiet. Luo Zhen playfully and charmingly conveyed this to Kurt, who nodded his head smiling and said, "Well, yes."

. . . .

Elsa is like a part of the Broyde family. Even the rabbi, Meylekh Broyde, speaks with her as if she were his sister. Little Mendele laughs and buries his hands in her blond hair while Malkele, Mrs. Broyde, tells her a great deal about her home and her parents in the small Polish town. And the yeshiva students speak with Elsa openly and in Yiddish, look at her like she is a girl of the family. Khayimke is fond of her company, calling her always without pretenses, "Elsa, Elsa. . . . "

Khayimke is part of the younger crowd of yeshiva students, and he looks as if he had just been weaned from his mother's apron strings. He is an elegant young man. Well dressed with a coat and hat, Khayimke is twenty-four years old. And as he hangs around, Elsa blushes crimson because she feels that Khayimke has something on his mind.

. . . .

Kurt arrived at his parents with a basket of fruit and with a special gift for each. He did not lack money. When he saw how they enjoyed the presents, he decided to tell them that they needed to prepare themselves for his wedding.

"Meaning what?" all three exclaimed wondering.

"I have a girl, Luo Zhen is her name, she is Chinese and we shall be married."

Robert was hurt to the quick. He was not about to give his agreement because, he decided, Kurt must marry a European girl. Robert's pain became a cough, his face turned red as if bathed in blood, and he couldn't utter a single word.

"Shame on you, Kurt," Elsa said accusingly to her brother. "Be ashamed of yourself for not marrying a Jewish girl. To have a wife who is not Jewish is a sin. You will never leave hell."

Father and Mother looked oddly at Elsa, as if she were somewhat out of her senses. Suddenly they did not recognize her. When Kurt left the room, banging the door as he did, Robert, the father, exclaimed, "Terrible!" [*furchtbar*].

And Grete, the mother, added, "Terrible!"

. . . .

Meylekh Broyde talked with Malkele, telling her that it would be a good deed to snatch Elsa from the Germans' room and to marry her to one of their boys. Malkele considered this a great idea. She always thought of Elsa as being lonely.

Among the yeshiva students were men who, for the love of Torah study, had remained bachelors, did not marry, and were now older Jews. Khayimke, however, belonged to the younger crowd; he was only twenty-four years old and by far the most elegant among the younger men. He liked to dress well. If it must be a yeshiva student, then fathers of girls want a young one and especially one like Khayimke. He was known in all Jewish rooms; Malkele once jokingly asked him, "Khayimke, which one of the girls will you choose?"

"I will tell you the truth, Malkele," Khayimke answered in a whisper, "among all of them I like our Elsa best. Yes Malkele, Elsa has captured my heart."

Malkele thought about this a lot, and later she talked it over with her husband. Meylekh Broyde liked the idea of the match very much.

"I think you should talk with her father," said Malkele to Khayimke.

"I don't know him."

"But he knows you."

"If that's the case you should speak with Elsa. I think so."

Malkele grabbed Elsa with both hands and hugged her to her heart. She had a welcome message for Elsa.

"What Malkele?" asked Elsa anxiously.

"Do you want Khayimke for a fiancé?"

Elsa turned pale and red. One color down, the other up. Tears glistened in her eyes and, putting her blond head on Malkele's shoulder, she had a good cry. So much happiness in one minute.

That very same day Meylekh Broyde went to Elsa's parents. When it comes to a good deed one does not procrastinate. Robert immediately recognized Elsa's "rabbi." He moved a chair close and said loudly, "Please be seated."

Rabbi Broyde spoke to Robert slowly so that he would more easily understand his Yiddish. "There is a very nice young man from a good Jewish family. We also know Elsa very well. We are convinced, my wife and I, that this is a very suitable match." It was difficult for him, that is for Broyde, to make sure that Elsa's father understood his Yiddish, understood it well.

"Herr Stein," Meylekh Broyde continued, "as a religious Jew, I want to tell you that as things are at the present time with Jews, there should be more weddings . . . is that not right?"

Broyde and his talk made a good impression on Elsa's father.

"But, Herr Broyde," Robert Stein asked, "what is the occupation of the young man?"

"He is in the yeshiva," Broyde answered simply.

"What, a yeshiva student?"

"Yes."

"Do you think, Herr Rabbi, that my Elsa will be agreeable? You know Elsa."

"Certainly," Broyde answered, "my wife already spoke with her."

"Oh, I see." Robert nodded his head. But he soon softened, although he had to say, "A wedding, Herr Rabbi, is connected with many expenses."

"No worries on that score," Broyde calmed him.

In fact, Robert had often heard that the yeshiva students were rich people.

"What is his name?"

"Khayimke, Khayimke Gutman. Please Mr. Stein, come to me in the evening and see Khayimke for yourself and we will continue to talk."

After Broyde left Robert felt as if he had smoke in his head: Elsa and a yeshiva student. . . .

"Grete, what do you say?"

"And what do you say?" she answered in turn.

In the evening, Robert Stein went to the Broyde family. This was the first time he had been invited to visit anyone since he came to Shanghai. The table was covered with a white tablecloth. Plates with fruit and delicacies of all kinds were on the table. All in his honor. Robert's mustache now looked softer, more sentimental. He liked Khayimke almost at first sight. An excellent boy.

"Are you a rabbi?" Robert Stein asked Khayimke.

"In time," Broyde quickly interjected.

"And what says Elsa? Where is she? She is almost always here with you!"

Elsa came to her father like a grown-up lady who knows well enough that it is her fate that is being decided.

"Papa," said Elsa, "you can admit it, yes, yes."

The Broydes and Khayimke smiled good-naturedly upon hearing her blessing. Elsa too smiled, even if her face changed color from white to red.

Elsa's father, Robert Stein, shook Khayimke's hand. Robert looked as though he were in seventh heaven. Broyde filled glasses with whisky and they drank to life and wished one another good luck.

. . . .

In addition to putting up a *mezuzah* [parchment scroll in a container] on his in-laws' doorpost, Khayimke also made sure Elsa and her parents had kosher food and decent meals at noon. He arranged for them to eat in the kitchen of the religious Jews, where the food was both kosher and tasty. Moreover, those who ate there sat at tables, and waiters brought plates with food.

"Excellent [*fabelhaft*]," Robert and Grete said admiringly. They were surprised, had no words, so delighted were they, and did not know whether to be grateful to Khayimke or to the people, so that no one would be disappointed. Robert and Grete realized that Elsa's bridegroom was an important person. Hadn't they often heard that the yeshiva students were rich people?

Robert was now regarded as a respected person by the yeshiva people and rabbis. Everybody greeted him with a hearty "good morning." Some people even called him Rav Robert.

. . . .

The wedding was like those that once were had by the best Jews in the small towns. All the rabbis' wives and the wives of the yeshiva students came with the Broydes at the head. Hundreds of people, refugee rabbis and all the yeshiva students from the oldest to the youngest, were in the synagogue surrounding the wedding canopy. The bridegroom delivered a sermon and Elsa's father looked at him as if he were a trickster whose tricks are beyond understanding. He was especially surprised by the dancing, circle within circle and so fast, wild, and everybody sang. They caught the German in one of the circles, he was after all the bride's father, and forced him to dance, though he danced like a clod. But his face was red and glistened with sweat pouring from his forehead.

Kurt, Elsa's brother, came uninvited; neither his parents nor Elsa had asked him to join. Kurt had embarrassed them all and had insulted them. Strangers had told him about the wedding; therefore, he came alone and when he drank the first glass of whisky, he announced loudly, "The bride is my sister." When this was heard, someone grabbed him and pulled him into a circle. The bride's brother must dance and not stand there like a statue. Kurt turned round and round like a drunkard, stepping on strangers' feet so that they threw him out of the circle. He barely made it outside, where he vomited.

. . . .

Kurt and Luo Zhen came to visit. Actually it was Luo Zhen who brought Kurt. She could not endure any longer the shame in front of her father, mother, and neighbors because Kurt's parents were opposed to her. Luo Zhen remained standing at the door, as she dared not go closer to Kurt's father. Kurt spoke for her. From the few words that she understood and from his facial expressions, she recognized that he was asking his parents for kind-heartedness and forgiveness. If she also asked, it was silently. Her tears spoke for her.

"Why did you not ask me?" the father insisted.

"I am guilty, please forgive me."

"Grete, what do you say?"

"But he explained to you then." The mother defended her son.

"All right. Ask Luo Zhen to come to the table."

Suddenly, however, something happened. Robert hurriedly urged Kurt and the Chinese girl to leave the room immediately. He almost threw them out.

"Come again in about half an hour, come again."

Kurt and Luo Zhen did not understand what had happened. They left the room to wait somewhere. What happened was that through the window Robert saw Khayimke and Elsa, her head covered [as it was proper for married women], coming to see him. He was afraid, was Robert, to have the two couples meet.

"Welcome Khayimke, welcome Elsa," said Robert.

I end this collection with a story that shows that, despite hardships endured by the Shanghai Jews, life, indeed, goes on. Fishman's preface to the collection of stories from which "The Wedding" comes is dated 1947. Quite likely, however, the story was written earlier. It is a highly unusual one dealing with matters that were not discussed in newspaper articles at the time, nor in scholarly essays later. More than most other refugees, Fishman was apparently aware of the plight of the Chinese in the city, as he briefly sketched it in "Miniatures." In this story, the Chinese are also present, but he deals with more complex matters: the loss of parental authority due to exile, the bankruptcy of Jewish assimilation, and the search for more meaningful commitments by the younger generation. In addition, he touches on the relationships of the ethnic communities forced to live in close proximity to one another in Hongkou—the lanes (as shown in the frontispiece to this book)—and he takes a rather pessimistic view of bridging the Chinese-Jewish divide. Fishman points to the existence of these problems but does not offer solutions; they are hinted at so delicately that the reader may easily miss the implications.

The waning of parental authority is indicated at the very beginning of the story, when the father feels shame in front of his children. His shame is understandable, for he, the strong father figure, was unable to protect his family and to prevent their exile. He is unable to assert himself and to keep his family together; first his son leaves, refusing to move into the ghetto, then his daughter finds a warm and loving refuge with, of all people, Polish Jews. Robert, who had been a completely assimilated German Jew, never recovered his bearings in Shanghai; he is unable to make the kinds of adjustments demanded by his changed station in life and the changed situation.

The youngsters, Kurt and Elsa, on the other hand, are capable of remarkable flexibility in adversity. Kurt finds meaning in extensive entrepreneurial activity and in a relationship with a Chinese girl. Elsa finds fulfillment in the warm, lively, and probably very noisy surroundings of a Polish rabbi's family. Although Elsa's father is at first taken aback when a match is proposed between his daughter and a yeshiva student, he is soon reconciled when advantages to the match emerge. He need no longer go with his pot to the soup kitchen where unappetizing fare is doled out. Instead, Elsa's fiancé arranges meals for his in-laws in far better surroundings.

The couple's wedding, a huge affair, is arranged by the Orthodox community. Kurt and Luo Zhen will not be that lucky. Her parents are poor and do not approve of the foreign boyfriend; Elsa does not approve of a non-Jewish bride; Robert is apprehensive and, even if Fishman does not say this explicitly, the reader wonders whether Robert fears the loss of decent food if a non-Jewish woman were to enter the family. In the end, the author seems to indicate, Robert cannot overcome his shame, and there remain certain cultural and religious barriers that not even marriage—and love—can surmount. Not in Jewish Shanghai of the 1930s and '40s, nor even in today's global community.

Acknowledgments

Above all I must thank Paul Mendes-Flohr for enthusiastically endorsing the idea of translating some of those neglected and forgotten works from Shanghai. More than that, he read an earlier draft and made numerous useful suggestions on how to improve the text. It was he who persuaded me to include Meylekh Ravitch in this collection. During one of her visits to Jerusalem, when she was occupied with her own research, Barbara Johnson nonetheless found the time to read the entire manuscript. Her critical questions and stylistic suggestions are deeply appreciated. A major debt of gratitude is due Joshua Fogel. His comments, enthusiastic as well as critical, were both welcome and very much appreciated. In addition, I am especially grateful for his invaluable help in correcting my Yiddish transliterations.

While translating and trying to find information about the various writers who left Shanghai after 1945 for America, Australia, and Europe, I received much help from several people. At the very start of this project, Elli Joffe reminded me that if I translate poetry that rhymes in the original, I must use rhyme in the translation. Heeding his advice was not always easy, but he was right and I thank him for the suggestion. I am grateful to Peter Witting, Annie's son, for permission to reproduce these letters, for biographical information on Annie and on the Wilhelm and Witting families, and for patiently answering my questions in a personal communication of 8 September 2006 in which he recounted the 2006 "Shanghai Reunion." Shalom Eilati gave generously of his time and thorough knowledge of Yiddish to help with some of the more complicated verses. I am especially grateful to Dr. Eilati for transcribing portions of the diary of Yehoshua Rapoport, whose handwriting I was unable to decipher. Moreover, the translation of Yoni Fayn's poem, in particular, has benefited much from his sensitive reading. Itamar Livni's help with hard-to-find material in the National and University Library was indispensable. With singular energy he applied himself to ferreting out books and articles that I had thought were not available in Israel.

Finally, no expression of gratitude will suffice for Joan Hill's unflagging and skillful assistance. For her unsurpassed computer know-how, bibliographic detective work, and singular commitment to this project I am deeply grateful. In addition to specific citations, all of the biographies have benefited from her prowess at finding information in many and diverse sources. Without question, the biographical portions in this volume could not have been written without her unstinting help. Despite the distance (Joan lives in Cambridge, Massachusetts), and inevitable postal delays, she managed to frequently send much-needed materials. Her constant support saw me through the more difficult portions of the translating effort.

Special thanks are due to the research librarians in Widener Library, the Judaica Division and Government Information Services Harvard. Randolph Petilos's meticulous care and much-needed editorial advice, aside from the enormous help and encouragement he provided at all times, are deeply appreciated. Finally, my utmost gratitude to Michael Koplow for his superb editing from which this manuscript has greatly benefited. I am grateful to all these, and I am solely responsible for any inadequacies and shortcomings that remain.

Notes

Introduction

1. R. Shoshana Kahan, *In fayer un flamen: togbukh fun a yidisher shoyshpilerin* (In fire and flames: diary of a Jewish actress) (Buenos Aires: Tsentral farband fun poylishe yidn in Argentine, 1949), p. 283.

2. Yad Vashem Archives (YVA), 078/105, "Memoir of Annemarie Pordes," p. 52.

3. Central Archive for the History of the Jewish People, Jerusalem (CAHJP), DAL 48, Braverman to HIAS-ICA-EMIGDIRECT, Paris, December 13, 1933 (Yiddish letter).

4. *Israel's Messenger*, March 1, 1936. Karfunkel became a Chinese citizen on January 16, 1936.

5. Copy of a letter signed by Heydrich, January 31, 1939, in John Mendelsohn, ed., *The Holocaust: Selected Documents in Eighteen Volumes* (New York and London: Garland, 1982), vol. 6, pp. 202–203.

6. Frederic Wakeman, Jr., "Policing Modern Shanghai," *China Quarterly*, no. 115 (September 1988), p. 409.

7. Hanchao Lu, *Beyond the Neon Lights: Everyday Shanghai in the Early Twentieth Century* (Berkeley: University of California Press, 1999), p. 36.

8. This summary of the Shanghai administrative system is based on Robert W. Barnett, *Economic Shanghai: Hostage to Politics, 1937–1941* (New York: Institute of Pacific Relations, 1941), pp. 5–7. The Japanese were not among the treaty powers, having never acquired a concession in Shanghai.

9. The Russian diaspora everywhere in the twentieth century is estimated at between one and two million persons. The many cities in which people settled for longer or shorter periods of time are detailed in Karl Schlögel, ed., *Der grosse Exodus, die russische Emigration und ihre Zentren, 1917 bis 1941* (Munich: C.H. Beck, 1994).

10. Christian Henriot, " 'Little Japan' in Shanghai: An Insulated Community, 1875–1945," in Robert Bickers and Christian Henriot, eds., *New Frontiers: Imperialism's New Communities in East Asia, 1842–1953* (Manchester: Manchester University Press, 2000), p. 148.

11. For a detailed history of this important family, see Maisie Meyer, *From the*

Rivers of Babylon to the Whangpoo (Lanham: University Press of America, Inc., 2003), pp. 11–16.

12. Chiara Betta, "Myth and Memory: Chinese Portrayals of Silas Aaron Hardoon, Luo Jialing, and the Aili Garden Between 1924 and 1925," in Roman Malek, ed., *Jews in China, from Kaifeng . . . to Shanghai* (Sankt Augustin: Monumenta Serica Institute, 2000), p. 377.

13. Marie-Claire Bergère, "The Other China: Shanghai from 1919 to 1949," in Christopher Howe, ed., *Shanghai: Revolution and Development in an Asian Metropolis* (Cambridge: Cambridge University Press, 1981), pp. 7–9.

14. Leo Ou-fan Lee, *Shanghai Modern: The Flowering of Urban Culture in China, 1930–1945* (Cambridge, MA: Harvard University Press, 1999), p. 84.

15. Parks M. Coble, *Chinese Capitalists in Japan's New Order: The Occupied Lower Yangzi, 1937–1945* (Berkeley: University of California Press, 2003), p. 11.

16. The grim circumstances of Shanghai's refugees is ably recounted by Christian Henriot, "Shanghai and the Experience of War: The Fate of Refugees," *European Journal of East Asian Studies*, Vol. 5, no. 2 (September 2006), pp. 215–245.

17. The dire situation until the outbreak of the Pacific War is described by Frederic Wakeman, Jr., *The Shanghai Badlands, Wartime Terrorism and Urban Crime, 1937–1941* (Cambridge: Cambridge University Press, 1996).

18. Shanghai Municipal Police Files, Reel 17, D54422(c), Police Report files dated July 3, 7, 9, 15, 24, 31, 1939.

19. YVA, 078/85, Shanghai Municipal Archives, G. Godfrey Phillips, SMC secretary and commissioner general to German Jewish Aid Committee, London; HIAS-ICA-EMIGRATION Association, Paris; American Joint Distribution Committee, New York, December 23,1938.

20. Public Record Office, London (PRO), minutes, first page is missing.

21. PRO, FO371/24079 (22652), W519, 5, Foreign Office cable to the Ambassador in Shanghai, January 10, 1939.

22. YVA, 078/88, Shanghai Municipal Archives, Police Report, sent to the SMC secretary and commissioner general, May 24, 1940.

23. YVA, 078/21, H. (Peter) Eisfelder, "Chinese Exile: My Years in Shanghai and Nanking 1938 to 1947," 2nd rev. ed., 1985, and YVA, 078/70, "Shanghai 1938–1949," Al Zunterstein tape.

24. Michael Philipp and Wilfried Seywald, eds., Hans Schubert and Mark Siegelberg, *"Die Masken Fallen"—"Fremde Erde," Zwei Dramen aus der Emigration nach Shanghai 1937–1947* (Hamburg: Hamburger Arbeitsstelle für deutsche Exilliteratur, 1996).

25. Lothar Briger, "Emigration und kuenstlerische Produktivitaet," *Shanghai Herald*, special edition, April 1946, p. 18.

26. Wolfgang Fischer, "Wir und Shanghai's Judenschaft," *Shanghai Woche*, no. 9 (August 1, 1942), p. 1.

27. Guy Stern, *Literarische Kultur im Exil: Gesammelte Beiträge zur Exilforschung, 1989–1997* (Literary culture in exile: Collected essays in the German-speaking emigration after 1933 [1989–1997]) (Dresden: Dresden University Press, 1998), p. 18.

28. YIVO Institute, HIAS-HICEM I, MKM 15.57, 15 B-24, The Jewish Community of Kobe, Committee for Assistance to Refugees, Kobe, J. Epstein to HICEM, Lisbon, August 18, 1941, p. 8.

29. "Official Inauguration of SACRA," *Our Life* [English page of *Nasha Zhizn*], no. 41, April 2, 1943. Guests of honor were Tsutomu Kubota and M. Kano.

30. JDC, file 739, "J.D.C. Aid to Refugee Yeshivoth Students and Rabbis from Poland," April 2, 1944.

31. JDC, file 738, "Memorandum on Emigration from Lithuania," signed Moses A. Leavitt, January 17, 1941.

32. This is argued by Leyzer Kahan, "Nisim oyf unzer vanderveg" (Miracles on our journey), *In veg*, November 1941, p. 7.

33. Zwartendijk merely wrote in the passports that a visa was not required for either Surinam or Curaçao. Samuel N. Adler, *Against the Stream* (n.p., Jerusalem, 2001), p. 30.

34. CAHJP, DAL 87, Birman to Reich Association, June 10, 1940. The ships were handled by the Kitonihon Kisenkaisha Company.

35. Joseph Rotenberg, *Fun Varshe biz Shanghai: notitsn fun a palit* (From Warsaw to Shanghai: a refugee's notes) (Mexico: Shlomo Mendelsohn Fund, at the Company for Culture and Help, 1948), p. 339.

36. "Volna polskich emigrantov v Shanchai" (New wave of Polish emigrants in Shanghai), *Nasha Zhizn*, no. 1 (August 29, 1941), p. 9.

37. JDC, file 462, EastJewCom to M. Speelman, August 25, 1941, and cable from Margolis to JDC, October 9, 1941.

38. "Razyasnemiye yaponskich vlastey otnositelno prozhivaniya bezhentsev v Hongkew" (Japanese authorities explain policy on immigrants living in Hongkew)," *Nasha Zhizn*, no. 20 (September 12, 1941), p. 11. The Americans froze Japanese assets in July 25, 1941, in retaliation for the Japanese move into Vietnam, according to Joseph C. Grew, *Ten Years in Japan* (New York: Simon and Schuster, 1944), p. 408.

39. JDC, file 461, Executive Committee minutes, May 21, 1941.

40. Hillel Levine, *In Search of Sugihara: The Elusive Japanese Diplomat Who Risked His Life to Rescue 10,000 Jews from the Holocaust* (New York: Free Press, 1996). Notwithstanding the title, Levine states in pp. 285–286 n. 7 that this is merely a "reasonable estimate."

41. YIVO Institute, HIAS-HICEM I, MKM 15.57, 15 B-24, The Jewish Community of Kobe, Committee for the Assistance of Refugees, Kobe, J. Epstein to HICEM, Lisbon, August 18, 1941, 9 pp.

42. *Der dibek* was reviewed in *Undzer lebn* [Yiddish page of *Nasha Zhizn*], no. 30, November 28, 1941. *Mirele Efros* was announced in *Undzer lebn*, no. 40, February 6, 1942. It was apparently not reviewed.

43. YVA, 11.728, Reel 16, M. Siegel to the American JDC, August 26, 1945.

44. Bernard Wasserstein, "Ambiguities of Occupation, Foreign Resisters, and Collaborators in Wartime Shanghai," in Yeh Wen-hsin, ed., *Wartime Shanghai* (London: Routledge, 1998), p. 26.

45. YVA, 11.728, Reel 16, Siegel, ibid.

46. I borrow this apt phrase from Thomas L. Jeffers, "God, Man, the Devil— and Thomas Mann," *Commentary*, 120, no. 4 (November 2005), p. 78.

47. Birgit Linder, "China in German Translation: Literary Perceptions, Canonical Texts, and the History of German Sinology," in Leo Tak-hung Chan, ed., *One into Many: Translation and the Dissemination of Classical Chinese Literature* (Amsterdam: Rodopi, 2003), p. 273.

48. Mordechai Holtzblat, *Konfutsius, zayn lebn un tetikeyt* (Confucius: his life and work), (Warsaw: Oryent, n.d.); and Laozi, R. Zeligman, trans., *Der bukh funem getlikhen gezets* (The book of the divine law), (Berlin: Klal, 1923).

49. Jacob Dinezohn, *Di velt geshikhte* (World history), (Warsaw: Pen Club, 1937); Nahum Bomse, *Iberdikhtungen fun Li-Tai-pe (699–762)* (Rewritten poetry by Li Bai), (Warsaw: Pen Club, 1937).

50. Peretz Hirshbein, "Harbin," *Der Moment*, 36 (February 11, 1927), pagination missing on microfilm; "Kanton," *Der Moment*, 90 (April 29, 1927), p. 6.

51. For example, "Iber a milyon dakhloze khinezer" (Over a million homeless Chinese), *Haynt*, no. 260 (November 12, 1937), p. 2.

52. Irene Eber, "Translation Literature in Modern China: The Yiddish Author and His Tale," *Asian and African Studies* (Jerusalem), vol. 8, no. 3 (1972), pp. 291–314.

53. Meylekh Ravitsh, "A riksha shtarbt in a Shanghaier fartog" (A rickshaw [coolie] dies on a Shanghai dawn), in *Kontinentn un okeanen* (Continents and oceans) (Warsaw: Literarishe bleter, 1937), pp. 44–46.

54. The following account is based on Melech Rawitsch [Meylekh Ravitch], Armin Eidherr, trans., *Das Geschichtenbuch meines Lebens, Auswahl* (Salzburg: Otto Müller Verlag, 1996), pp. 225–235, which consists of translated selections from Ravitch's autobiography.

55. Meylekh Ravitch, *Kontinentn un okeanen* (Warsaw: Literarishe bleter, 1937), pp. 44–46.

56. A description of Ravitch's China travel and travelogue, a typewritten manuscript in Yiddish, are in Irene Eber, "Meylekh Ravitch in China: A Travelogue of 1935," in Monika Schmitz-Eman, ed., *Transkulturelle Rezeption und Konstruktion, Festschrift für Adrian Hsia* (Heidelberg: Sinchron, 2004), pp. 103–117.

57. Jewish National and University Library, Jerusalem, Ravitch Collection, file 2:375, 145.

58. Annie's letter of July 1939 is in the Irene Eber Collection, Yad Vashem Archives (078/1).

59. Irene Eber Collection, Yad Vashem Archives (078/16).

60. This brief account is based on Wilfried Seywald, *Journalisten im Shanghaier Exil 1939–1949* (Vienna: Wolfgang Neugebauer Verlag, 1987), pp. 238–239, and Humphrey McQueen, *Social Sketches of Australia, 1880–2001* (Queensland: University of Queensland Press, 2004), rev. ed., p. 231.

61. Varro apparently did not lose his sure touch, though writing in English. See "The Australian Correspondent," *Observer*, vol. 3, no. 7, April 2, 1960, pp. 13–15.

62. *Shanghai Woche*, no. 1 (March 30, 1939), p. 3.

63. Werner Vordtriede, "Vorläufige Gedanken zu einer Typologie der Exilliteratur," in Wulf Koepke and Michael Winkler, eds., *Exilliteratur 1933–1945* (Darmstadt: Wissenschaftliche Buchgesellschaft, 1989), p. 38.

64. "American Seminary to Ready Local Jews for Life in the U.S.," *China Press*, August 31, 1946, pp. 5 and 12.

65. Biographical detail is contained in Weiyan Meng, "Willy Tonn: 'The Fighting Scholar' of Shanghai," *Sino-Judaica: Occasional Papers of the Sino-Judaic Institute*, vol. 2 (1995), pp. 111–128.

66. *Der Mitarbeiter*, no. 6, December 27, 1940, p. 6. Harvard College Library, Judaica Collection, Reel 96-2702 26061.

67. Irene Eber Collection, Yad Vashem Archives (078/1).

68. On the issue of culture shock, there is the essay by Helga Embacher and Margit Reiter, "Schmelztiegel Shanghai?—Begegnung mit dem 'Fremden,'" *Zwischenwelt*, vol. 18, no. 1 (February 2001), pp. 40–45.

69. Wilfried Seywald, *Journalisten im Shanghaier Exil, 1939–1949* (Vienna: Wolfgang Neugebauer Verlag, 1987), p. 359.

70. *Der Mitarbeiter*, no. 6, December 27, 1940, Harvard College Library, Judaica Collection, Reel 96-2702 26061.

71. Langston Hughes, *I Wonder as I Wander: An Autobiographical Journey* (New York: Hill and Wang, 1956), p. 251.

72. Shanghai's dance hall phenomenon is ably described by Leo Ou-fan Lee in *Shanghai Modern: The Flowering of a New Urban Culture in China, 1930–1945* (Cambridge, MA: Harvard University Press, 1999), pp. 23–29.

73. *New York Times*, November 2, 1995, and *Dei'ah veDibur*, January 28, 2004.

74. JDC, file 462, "List of Recent Arrivals," August 30, 1941; Simkhoni arrived on the same ship as Yosl Mlotek and, like Mlotek, is not listed among yeshiva arrivals.

75. "Dray lender hobn mikh oisgeshpign," *Undzer lebn*, no. 20 (September 12, 1941).

76. This poem and the remarks about it have appeared in German translation by Dorthe Seifert. Irene Eber, "Auf einer einsamen Insel, Jiddische Dichter in Shanghai," *Jüdischer Almanach, 2001/5761 des Leo Baeck Instituts*, pp. 163–64.

77. Lewin's biographical sketch is based on the brief entry in Werner Röder, et al., eds., *Biographisches Handbuch der deutschsprachigen Emigration nach 1933* (Munich and New York: K.G. Saur, 1980), Vol. 1, pp. 440–41.

78. "Mehr Licht," *Die Laterne*, no. 1, June 14, 1941, p. 4. YIVO Institute for Jewish Research, Reel Y-2003-1854.8.

79. Personal communication, July 7, 2006.

80. Y. Rapoport, *Der mahut fun dikhtung un ir sotsiale funktsye* (The very essence of poetry and its social function), (Shanghai: Elenberg, 1941), pp. 3–5.

81. Meylekh Ravitch, *Mayn leksikon* (My lexicon) (Tel Aviv: Veltrat far yidish un yidisher kultur, 1982), vol. 6, p. 282. Also, *Leksikon fun der nayer yidisher literatur* (Biographical Dictionary of Modern Yiddish Literature), vol. 8, columns 392–95 (New York: Congress for Jewish Culture, Inc., 1956–1981), 8 vols.

82. "Ot azoy hoibt zikh dos on . . . "(yidishe kultur-arbeit in Shanghai), *In veg*, compilation (November 1941), pp. 9–14. YIVO Institute for Jewish Research, Reel Y-2003-1855.

83. Leksikon fun der nayer yidisher literatur, vol. 6, columns 2–3, and a tape recording from May 4, 1994.

84. The Bund refers to the secular Jewish socialist and workers' party. Its members were stongly Yiddishist.

85. The arrival in Shanghai is listed in JDC, file 462, "List of Recent Arrivals."

86. "Joseph Mlotek, Yiddish educator and writer, dies at 81,"*Jewish News Weekly of Northern California*, July 14, 2000.

87. "Dem gevayn fun mayn mamen," YIVO Institute for Jewish Research, Reel Y-2003-1855, *In veg*, compilation (November 1941), pp. 17–18.

88. *Undzer lebn*, no. 39 (January 30, 1942).

89. *Leksikon fun der nayer yidisher literatur*, vol. 8, column 370.

90. "Zun in netzn," Judaica Collection, Harvard College Library, Reel 99.774 C4069, *Di yidishe shtime fun vaytn mizrekh*, August 1942, p. 6.

91. *Undzer lebn*, no. 38 (January 23, 1942).

92. A portion of the poem and these remarks about it have appeared in a German translation by Dorthe Seifert in Irene Eber, "Auf einer einsamen Insel," pp. 167–69.

93. "Der pflichtbewusste Maurer," Shanghai Municipal Police Files, Reel 18, D5422(o), submitted to the SMP by L. Margolis and M. Siegel, March 17, 1942, for a cabaret evening to be held March 21, 1942.

94. Shanghai Municipal Police Files, Reel 18, D5422(o).

95. Jacob Fishman's biography is based on *Leksikon fun der nayer yidisher literatur*, Vol. 7, p. 395.

96. Fishman, *Farvoglte yidn* (Shanghai: J. M. Elenberg, 1948; reprinted in Amherst: National Yiddish Book Center, 1999). Steven Spielberg Digital Yiddish Library, no. 10847.

97. *Undzer lebn*, no. 40 (February 6, 1942).

98. *Undzer lebn*, no. 99 (March 26, 1943). Also, "Vart oif mir" (Wait for me), *Undzer vort*, collection, 1945, pp. 42–43. YIVO Institute for Jewish Research, Reel Y-2003-1855.9.

99. This poem together with the remarks about it have appeared in a German translation by Dorthe Seifert in Irene Eber, "Auf einer einsamen Insel," pp. 165–66.

100. This unpublished diary is held in the Archive of the Jewish National and University Library, Jerusalem (Arc. 4°, 410).

101. "Szpilki, u mnie nie!," *Echo Szanghajskie*, no. 11 (July–August 1944), p. 2.

102. Lion Feuchtwanger, *Ein Buch nur für meine Freunde* (Frankfurt am Main: Fischer Taschenbuch Verlag, 1984), p. 535.

103. Fayn's biography is based on Berl Kagan, ed., *Leksikon fun yidish-shraibers* (Lexicon of Yiddish writers) (New York: R. Ilman-Kohen, 1986), p. 440, and Julia Goldman, "To Paint History," *Jewish Week*, July 11, 2003.

104. Yoni Fain [Fayn], *A tlie unter di shtern* (A gallows under the stars) (Mexico City: Di shtime, 1947).

105. Yehoshua Rapoport, diary entry for July 18, 1943. Arc. 4 ° 410, the Jewish National and University Library.

106. YIVO Institute for Jewish Research, Reel Y-2003-1855.9. *Undzer vort*, collection, 1945, pp. 27–30.

107. "Ein Affe wurde Mensch." I thank Dr. Ruth Kollani for making the original of the poem available to me.

108. *Leksikon fun der nayer yidisher literatur*, Vol. 8, columns 24–25.

109. Alfred Dreifuss, "Mirele Efros, von Jakob Gordin," *Shanghai Herald*, May 7, 1946, p. 3.

110. R. Shoshana Kahan, *In fayer un flamen: togbukh fun a yidisher shoyshpilerin* (Buenos Aires: Tsentral farband fun poylishe yidn in Argentine, 1949).

111. Jonas Turkov (1898–?) and his wife must have been close friends of the Kahans. He was an actor and writer and his wife was an actress. They left Poland in 1945 and came to the U.S. in 1947. For Jonas Turkov's biography, see *Leksikon fun der nayer yidisher literatur*, Vol. 4, columns 58–60.

112. This according to the unpublished paper by Chang Shoou-Huey, "Eine jiddische Künstlerin im Exil in Shanghai während des Zweiten Weltkriegs—Rose Shoshana und ihr Tagebuch 'In Fajer un Flamen.'" Several entries from 1941 and 1942 were translated by Chang Shoou-Huey into German, "Rose Shoshana und ihr Tagebuch 'In fajer un flamen,' eine jüdische Künstlerin im Exil in Shanghai," *Zwischenwelt*, Vol. 18, no. 1 (February 2001), pp. 52–57.

113. YIVO Institute for Jewish Research, Reel Y-2003-1854.1, *The Shanghai Herald*, no. 10, March 11, 1946, p. 4.

114. Werner Vordtriede, "Vorläufige Gedanken zu einer Typologie der Exilliteratur," in Wulf Koepke and Michael Winkler, eds., *Exilliteratur 1933–1945* (Darmstadt: Wissenschaftliche Buchgesellschaft, 1989), p. 38.

115. Jacob H. Fishman, *Farvoglte yidn* (Homeless Jews) (Shanghai: J. M. Elenberg, 1948). Reprinted in Steven Spielberg Digital Yiddish Library, no. 10847 (Amherst: National Yiddish Book Center, 1999), pp. 39–52.

Index of Names